The Art of Storytelling

Telling Truths through Telling Stories

Amy E. Spaulding

THE SCARECROW PRESS, INC.
Lanham • Toronto • Plymouth, UK
2011

Published by Scarecrow Press, Inc.
A wholly owned subsidiary of The Rowman & Littlefield Publishing Group, Inc.
4501 Forbes Boulevard, Suite 200, Lanham, Maryland 20706
http://www.scarecrowpress.com

Estover Road, Plymouth PL6 7PY, United Kingdom

British Library Cataloguing in Publication Information Available

Library of Congress Cataloging-in-Publication Data
Spaulding, Amy E., 1944–
   The art of storytelling : telling truths through telling stories / Amy E. Spaulding.
       p. cm.
   Includes bibliographical references and index.
   ISBN 978-0-8108-7776-4 (hardback : alk. paper) — ISBN 978-0-8108-7777-1
(ebook)
   1. Storytelling. I. Title.
   LB1042.S675 2011
   372.67'7—dc22   2010039697

♾™ The paper used in this publication meets the minimum requirements of
American National Standard for Information Sciences—Permanence of
Paper for Printed Library Materials, ANSI/NISO Z39.48-1992.

Printed in the United States of America

To all the storytellers and students
who have taught me so much,
and to those of the future,
including you.

Good-bye, and thanks, to both Norman Horrocks, who introduced me
to library school and later to Scarecrow Press, and Augusta Baker, who
introduced me to storytelling at the New York Public Library, and in
whose honor I chose the storyteller for the cover. Augusta loved owls,
and this Zuni storyteller from about 1900 is quite rare in portraying a
storyteller as other than human.

Truth nor story can be written in stone;
each dies when petrified.

Contents

Part I: Telling Truth, Telling Stories

1   Teaching Storytelling and Teaching through Storytelling   3

2   Welcome and Congratulations   7

3   Celebrate the Joy of Storytelling   13

Part II: How to Become a Storyteller

4   A Living Art: How Does One Learn Stories?
It Is Worth the Effort   25

5   Types of Stories   35

6   Selecting a Story, and Version, to Tell   43

7   Building a Program   55

8   Performance Issues   69

9   Interacting with the Audience   75

10   The Business of Storytelling   81

Part III: Why Bother Learning and Telling Stories?

11   Storytelling versus Storycrafting: Traditional versus
Current Forms   91

12   The Ethics and Psychology of Storytelling   101

13 The Energy of Storytelling   109

14 Storytelling in Times of Anxiety and Change   116

15 The Storyteller's Responsibility to the Audience:
        Choosing Stories You Trust   124

Part IV: Farewell

16 Storytelling Values, the Value of Storytelling   133

Appendix A: Storiography   139

Appendix B: Story Collections   179

Appendix C: Webliography—Web Sites Useful to
            Storytellers and Students   189

Selected Bibliography   195

Index   203

About the Author   209

Part I

TELLING TRUTH, TELLING STORIES

Teaching Storytelling and Teaching through Storytelling

The technique of any art is sometimes apt to dampen, as it were, the spark of inspiration in a mediocre artist; but the same technique in the hands of a master can fan that spark into an unquenchable flame.

—Joseph Jasser[1]

Jasser's warning can be accurate—but what does it mean to a teacher of the art of storytelling? How do you know your students and their abilities before experiencing their talent? I remember well how my professor father quelled any hope I ever had of daring to write by criticizing my grammar. He meant well, and he was accurate in his assessment, but it made me very anxious, so that writing still requires an act of will. That same man also told me wonderful stories at bedtime; he dismissed his teaching role and had fun. Now I can talk a blue streak, but putting words on paper still scares me. My experience of one was that of an intellectual lesson and the other as a gift, which begs the question: how do you teach an art? How do you offer helpful advice that will assist artists to grow without dampening their enthusiasm?

All you can do is *care*, hope for the best, and ask each person to take responsibility for his or her own learning. As my tai chi teacher says, "You cannot teach by humiliation. You can dominate or indoctrinate, but you cannot stimulate growth. That, as with plants, takes sun and water and time alone in the dark."[2] This is very similar to what happens when you tell stories: although you don't know how they will be interpreted, you do know that occasionally you will be surprised by the response.

Storytelling is very much in fashion right now, which is both good and bad. Good because it is getting attention, bad because it is being experimented with by some who do not understand or respect its power and end up misusing it.[3]

The issue of lying within storytelling is something that will appear later; it involves storytelling that tricks the audience, not for entertainment or teaching but to serve the selfish ends of the trickster; a fair number of stories deal with just that. The old sideshow barker and the television huckster on infomercials epitomize this negative role of trying to manipulate with story. Much commercial advertising and certainly politics uses story, sometimes legitimately, to make something clear and sometimes to lead an audience to an "inescapable" conclusion. The issue is introduced here just to ensure that story's power is recognized.

Entertainment is a requirement for successful storytelling. No story works without it; otherwise it becomes a lecture. Most of us have experienced such non-storytelling, so I won't belabor the point. We are living in an age of mistrust, and this extends to education, where to a student learning often feels like letting the teachers "win" by allowing "their" values to be superimposed on "mine." In contrast to formal education, storytelling allows a listener to allow an idea to grow naturally to fit the hearer.

The other idea that should be introduced at the very beginning is that story is an evanescent art. Truth, like story, cannot be written in stone, for it dies when it is solidified. The first person to write down the Veda (Hindu sacred scriptures) was called "the butcher of the Veda" because he trapped the words on paper, rather than letting them be alive and free as sound. This effect is evident in the fact that older, written versions of stories often lose their appeal. This also relates to why novels are different from oral stories, why films are different from both, and why online storytelling is different from in-person storytelling and will probably require new terminology to describe it. A musical analogy would be the difference between going to a concert and listening to a CD; and both are very different from reading a score.

Why tell stories? Ideally, storytellers are selling hope. The psychiatrist Milton Erickson, who used stories as his method of therapy, telling the beginnings and letting the patient choose the ending, said that he could prevent a patient's depression by getting that patient to accept that a 90 percent success rate was a good result. The patient came to accept that demanding perfection was unrealistic and foolish. In other words, it is silly to expect to always win, but one can always gain from any experience. In traditional story terms, this can be seen in the pattern of the third son: the first two were so self-important and determined to succeed that they missed opportunities, while the third son was open to possibilities and willing to take a chance—success came as a by-product of trying something unexpected.

Although it may feel like it, disappointment is not defeat—it is just not success *yet.* Learning lies in recognizing disappointment as a local rather than a cosmic event, believing that hope can sanely remain. Hope makes a better companion than despair, regardless of how or where a journey aims or ends up. Story supports hope: it gives courage to fight when needed, laughter when the unexpected happens, and a kind of verbal sanctuary of wisdom to ponder in times of quiet. Everything is transitory.

If a listener can learn that living is not about establishing self-importance but about becoming comfortable with reality and can see that "truth" can come in many forms, then that person may become content with life as it is, rather than expecting it to meet all desires and provide constant stimulation. Maybe the fate of the third son can still convince people that it is worth trying, without their being conscious of the lesson as a lesson. And whether it works or not, we can still have fun telling his story. *We are storytellers, not therapists or instructors; we tell what we love and listener beware: you are responsible for any meaning you attach to the tale.*

So let's prepare for giving entertainment to audiences, not for perfection. And let's remain aware of the joy that comes with storytelling, for both teller and listener. It is this joy that makes the effort well worthwhile.

> There are painters who transform the sun into a yellow spot, but there are others who with the help of their art and intelligence transform a yellow spot into sun.
>
> —Pablo Picasso[4]

EXERCISE

Are there any "stories" that have shaped your life or those of your family? And, yes, religion is one of the biggest and most important stories in many lives.

NOTES

1. In Michael Checkhov, *To the Actor: On the Technique of Acting* (New York: Harper & Row, 1953).

2. Maggie Newman, personal communication, January 24, 2010.

3. This reminds me of the wonderful film, *The Queen* (2006), in which Helen Mirren portrays Queen Elizabeth struggling to deal with the people's reaction to Princess Diana's death and the change in their feelings toward the royal family since her youth in World War II. I hope storytelling can remain relevant, even with the changes in media and society.

4. "News to Amuse," *North Beverly, Beverly Farms Manchester* (MA) *Free Coffee News*, December 14, 2009.

CHAPTER 2

Welcome and Congratulations

The rise and fall of the storyteller's voice expresses the heartbeat of the Earth Mother, Gaia.[1]

Welcome and congratulations. You are a storyteller! Each of us is a storyteller from the moment we are born and cry out our first sounds: "Here I am! Where am I?" Perhaps it is not in formal language, but it is an easily understandable communication, telling the story of life.

It is part of the legacy of being human. A recent student mentioned that her autistic son had announced with his vocabulary cards that he wanted pizza for supper. When she went to the refrigerator to get the frozen pizza, he communicated with frustration: No! . . . shoe . . . car . . . pizza!

It was a simple tale, but he was showing his imagined desired future for the family evening. Her recounting it was definitely telling a story, since she was addressing a class to convince them of the value of providing books and programs for children like her son. And my telling it is a third level of the same story. Again, the purpose is trying to convince an audience of something's value by retelling a story.

There is no guarantee that any particular story will be interesting to you or that a particular storyteller will be a good teller, but that is a different issue and probably related to why you bought this book.

Now, not every communication is in story format, or intended as such, but most of our speech is related to story in some way. This book is about formal storytelling, which is something a little more closely defined.

Let us deal with one of the major issues immediately. What is storytelling? As opposed to public speaking, preaching, teaching, acting, or declaiming/elocution. This last is out of fashion, but I had a few classmates in elementary school who learned how to recite pieces for an audience, and I will never forget the strap one of them showed me, which was used as punishment if she did not do well. Please do not expect that kind of discipline from me. If you succeed, wonderful, I will be very proud of your success, but it is your choice whether or not to try and how much effort to put in.

If you want to work with groups, Toastmasters teaches some of the skills of addressing numbers of people, also called public speaking. Such groups are available many places that storytelling groups are not present, so they can be very valuable in learning techniques useful to communicating with numbers of people. But recognize that their aim is different. It is like learning tap dancing instead of ballet or football instead of rugby. You learn similar skills that can be useful, but they are not the same. In this case, the aim of public speaking is convincing an audience, while yours as a storyteller is entertaining an audience and stimulating them to come to their own conclusions, if any.

Storytelling is a form of giving. It can be used to impose ideas, but that is something else. You can preach with story or sell with story or teach with story, but true storytelling should be a gift, with no demands that the story be interpreted in a particular way.

One of my students came up with an explanation of this belief. Maybe her words will help make it clear:

> One belief, one that many of us were brought up to believe, is that there is only one way to succeed. That comes by being the best, winning at whatever one takes on or becoming CEO—capturing something that is scarce that no one else can have. A second belief system is that there are many ways to succeed; for example, it is not better to be Picasso than to be Rembrandt or Mozart rather than Beethoven.
>
> This is the view of this class—that we each have something unique to offer. We each must strive to develop our own uniqueness. We are learning about the diversity of success, art, learning, spirituality, family life—all complex endeavors and all interesting because they are broad with no single goal. There are many ways to win at life. The role of the storyteller is like that of the coach, encouraging and poking us: to share our stories, our successes to see how we react to what we are listening to.
>
> Take for instance the story of Cinderella. Depending on how the story is being told each of us would have a different reaction. Each of us would have a different reaction and would prefer one of these versions of the

story depending on how the story is being told—each from the perspective of the teller. One might tell it with deep pathos leading us to cry at her trials and rage at her abusers. Another might lead us to hope for her survival and cheer her triumph and still another might tell it with humor, mocking the conventions of the fairy tale itself and leading us to laugh at our own expectations.

Each of us would have our own perspective and prefer one of these versions. However, the story is the same. Some like Mozart over Beethoven but all three storytellers have succeeded.[2]

My words would be a little different. The storyteller has the right to take a certain perspective on the story, indeed, the storyteller must do so in order to tell it well. But that perspective may be unconscious and there should be no intent to impose a reaction on the audience— share, yes, impose, no. You cannot help but have your own reaction to the story; how could you go through the effort of learning it without caring? That does not give you the right to determine how someone else should respond to it. You want to give fabric, rather than a "store-bought" dress, allowing the hearer to interpret it his own way rather than unthinkingly taking on the teller's way.

The storyteller is giving a gift, not trying to impose a perspective the way advertisers do, nor trying to impose the meaning of the story with unmistakable morals as a preacher would. That is why I separate storytelling from preaching, although there are many overlaps.

Having introduced religion, a good parallel can be made with the Protestant reformation—the interaction should be with "the word" not with someone else's "interpretation of the word." Whether or not the interpreter is "right," it is the hearer's responsibility to figure it out for him- or herself rather than depend on someone else to figure it out. (That is the theory, at least.)

It is not humanly possible to be a completely transparent teller, since it is an artistic act, but the best teller should be *translucent*, allowing the audience to interact with the story directly rather than imposing a perspective on its truth. The actor plays a different role, not a neutral one, by interpreting the individual character played and thus interposing both the character and the actor's selves on the story and audience.

Acting is also different from preaching. The preacher is trying to convince the hearer of an idea, while the actor is trying to portray what a character thinks rather than his or her own ideas. An actor is meant to interpret the character, while the storyteller is meant to be translucent, allowing the story to speak for itself and playing the role of vehicle for the story, not dominator of the audience. Both drama and storytelling began as sacred arts, and they are certainly closely related, but they are also quite different. The storyteller is more like the chorus of a Greek tragedy, not a participant like the actor, but one who is observing. Denzel Washington explains this well in an interview:

> Even though science fiction films like *The Book of Eli* tend to come complete with message to get across, Washington insists he's not interested in leading the audience by the hand. "It's not for me to say," he explains about what people should take away from the film. "I don't overanalyze it like, 'I want them to get this.' It shouldn't be as narrow as just what I think."[3]

The storyteller just tells the story. The audience is responsible for what they make of it.

Several years ago I copied something from the Storytel listserv, sent by someone from New Zealand, that also addresses this difference.

> I also get the other side of this from my "actor" friends, "You're not an actor, you're a storyteller." Seems sometimes one can't win.
>
> With experience both in acting and storytelling, the biggest differences I see are that
>
> 1. An actor usually (especially given the conventions of modern film and theater) is separated from the audience by what we call "the fourth wall"; *now* the actor *is* a character and is *not* interacting with the audience but rather is existing within the world he/she has created on the stage, which the audience is primarily observing but not actually participating in, except in the vicarious psychological sense every actor hopes for.
>   The storyteller, rather, is presenting the character to the audience and invites the audience through the fourth wall and into the world of the story, to participate sometimes quite actively. An actor friend once told me that he could never be a storyteller because he didn't like the audience so "close." He felt naked and vulnerable, like the audience was penetrating his space. I think he was talking about the fourth wall.
> 2. An actor plays one character at a time, usually, and without a narrator. A storyteller can be narrator, several characters, the setting, noise effects, provide imaginary props, all at the same time.
> 3. The actor is an element in the theater experience. The storyteller *is* the theater experience.[4]

At risk of overdoing it, here is yet another quote; this one from a fictional boy in the Dark Ages: "It was the sound of the tale-teller's voice, his words, and the skill of the skald [storyteller] at crafting images that each listener could picture in his own mind that gave stories their power. It would seem undignified and weak to have men stand in front of you posing and pretending, instead."[5] Here was someone who wanted the responsibility and power of setting the story his own way in his own mind, instead of having it interpreted by men "posing and pretending."

Often you will be startled to find that someone, having put a story you told through his or her own filters, comes up with a response that had not occurred to you. That's fine. It's like raising children. You don't know whether they will end up like you or completely different. Do you know the song "Plant a Radish, Get a Radish" from *The Fantasticks*?[6] The point of the song is that with vegetables one can count on the results, but with children "you are absolutely stuck" with what you get. The same is true with storytelling. You may tell a story that you think shows one thing and find that someone else took it in a very different direction. As I have said elsewhere, a student once told my class in young adult literature that she read *Animal Farm* knowing that it was about racism—something that she was dealing with in her new parochial school. Orwell was writing about communism, but she was reading it under different circumstances. One cannot help but view things through one's own experience.

I remember telling a love story and being very surprised when someone said it should be told in women's shelters to warn them about trusting men. I still don't understand that reaction, but the listener was entitled to her own conclusion. On another occasion, that same story brought a man to a turning point in his life. While telling it I heard someone softly crying, and a few days later the man who had been crying told me that it made him recognize that he had become abusive after coming back from war—something he had not been able to understand from therapy.

I once had a dance teacher who said: "I do the bee dance. I don't teach, I just say 'there is something to make honey from here.' What the other bee does with the information is none of my business."[7]

As a storyteller, you are responsible for telling stories that have value of some kind, whether by putting forth questions, supplying answers, or providing wonder, comfort, or plain old entertainment. Even if you are doing this for a living, you have a freedom from economic issues that most of the entertainment and education worlds would envy. And there is nothing wrong with doing it for the fun of it and leaving the analysis to others. You get to share wisdom rather than having to teach it or sell it.

EXERCISES

At this point, the most important thing to do is think about what stories you remember being told. They could be Bible stories or other stories with religious meaning, or they could be folk tales, lies, urban myths, advertisements, or romantic promises? Just think about what stories have stayed with you and why.

Then think about what stories you have told. Were they to encourage friends, entertain children you were taking care of, or for performance? Were they lies for entertainment, or those told to keep you out of trouble or to get someone else into trouble? Is there a pattern that gives you a clue about what might be a good type of story or type of audience to start with?

NOTES

1. A friend said this to me when I told her I was doing this book. It was such a lovely thought that I have included it. Feel free to share it. If it troubles you to think of Mother Earth as Gaia, feel free to shorten it to: The rise and fall of the storyteller's voice expresses the heartbeat of Mother Earth.

2. Elma Lugo, a student in my Wisdom of Storytelling class in the summer of 2008, wrote this in response to another student's confusion.

3. *New York Metro*, January 14, 2010, p. 18, www.metro.us.

4. Gordon.Hall@XTRA.CO.NZ in message dated March 9, 2001.

5. Judson Roberts, *The Road to Vengeance: Western Frankia Spring and Summer AD 845* (New York: HarperTeen, 2008), 295.

6. *The Fantasticks*, a musical, music by Harvey Schmidt, lyrics by Tom Jones, 1960.

7. Emily Conrad, October 2008. She also said: "You must be a great artist to be a good teacher; it means finding ways to explain things."

CHAPTER 3

Celebrate the Joy of Storytelling

It is the function of some people to be a lamp and some to be a mirror.

—Arne Nixon[1]

Storytelling enables us to be both lamp and mirror at the same moment. As a storyteller, we can present stories composed by someone else and thus reflect that person's idea; as listener, we can create the story in our own minds while mirroring back to the teller our experience of listening to the story. Either way, storytelling is joyful, full of life, and incorporating the joy of both the story and the event.

Stories can exhibit joy just by being fun—or by being meaningful in a way that makes the listener feel fulfilled even if the story is not a happy one. The joy comes not just from the story but also from connecting with others while sharing that story. It does not matter whether you are "sharing it out" by telling it or "sharing it in" by hearing the teller's words and creating it in your own mind. Either way, it is a shared activity, and there is an awareness of sharing with all those present that adds to the joy of a special occasion.

It is like going to a sports activity at which everyone supports the same team and everybody wins. Better than that, we are all on the same team. In our current era, everything seems to have been turned into competition, so this feels refreshing. Storytelling is, at the same time, an act of creation and also a connection with people from the past who we never knew. It feels meaningful, whether one is conscious of the connection with ages past or not. Feeling smug about it is completely optional, but it is clear that people feel something when they listen to told stories and that they enjoy it—and that their reactions are different from those elicited by reading novels while alone or by watching movies, which require a different kind of suspended disbelief because they are performances from the past that have been manufactured into a movie. The difference is that there is no interpersonal connection as there is with live drama or story.

Don't misinterpret the joy of storytelling. Telling is hard and requires considerable effort, and it can cause anxiety when done in public rather than in an informal setting with family or close friends. Telling in public is like going on a blind date with a bunch of people at once. Telling to adults or teenagers requires risking being viewed as an idiot in this age of easy cynicism.

The experience is rewarding and well worth the effort, but I don't want anyone to think that it happens by magic without stress or effort. There can be magic in the occasion of telling, but there isn't always—it can be a disappointment. Learning stories is hard work and so is telling. Today, more people are willing to prepare to run marathons than are willing to do the preparatory work of storytelling. But just as some find joy in running, there is a joy in telling stories and in knowing that you are part of something that has been a part of culture for as long as there has been any culture to be part of. That may make it sound as if it is "good and good for you," like vegetables, but the truth of the matter is that it is fun, like dessert, and like a good dessert, it requires a baker's effort.

What is the joy of storytelling? Well, part of it is just the fun of sharing a story—funny or otherwise—and part of it lies in the sense of having given a gift of value. Sitting around a dinner table with friends telling about shared experiences that get honed and shaped and decorated with many retellings is part of it, for that kind of storytelling is building community and reinforcing the bonds of shared experience—firsthand sharing, whether or not one participated in the event being turned into story. It is fun to embroider and embellish and relish memories.

Someone new to the group can listen and come to understand the values of the group and the way they value truth. Is it something rigid, static, and limited to strict fact, or can it be decorated and enjoyed? What can be played with and what is sacrosanct? Who can be ridiculed? Only ourselves or only enemies? Everybody? No one? After learning the rules, you can start telling your own stories that fit the rules of the occasion to introduce yourself, to establish that you are in accord with the group, or to prove your own importance.

In a way, I guess, it is the equivalent of dogs sniffing each other: (Sniff.) What group do you come from? (Sniff.) Where have you been? (Sniff.) What has nourished you? (Sniff.) How open are you to trusting?

Human interactions are a little different and such inquiries may or may not be expressed in words, but they are similar: Where are you from? What school did you go to? What do you do for a living? Do you have a sense of proportion, of humor, of occasion? What do you find funny? What topics are to be avoided? Politics? Sex? Religion? As society becomes more structured with children enlisted in sports teams rather than playing kick-the-can in the street, it is also being constantly deconstructed with people moving from place to place and having to establish new friendships often, and this kind of interaction becomes more important for establishing connection and identity, just the way sniffing is required when dog packs change.

Joy and humor are often connected, and storytellers can learn much from clowns. *Lighten Up: Survival Skills for People under Pressure*, a book written by a clown and his sister, Metcalf, who has worked with dying children as well as with business management, says that his work is based on an important idea that "humor and joy are skills, not the luck of the draw."[2] He speaks of three humor skills:

The ability to see the absurdity in difficult situations.
The ability to take yourself lightly while taking your work seriously.
A disciplined sense of joy in being alive.[3]

What does this have to do with formal storytelling? Beyond the obvious connections that clowning and storytelling are both performance arts intended to share value rather than impose it as an absolute and that each involves being willing to risk embarrassment in order to bring joy and pleasure to others, these humor skills remind us that storytelling is not just formal presentations but a normal part of everyday life, something that everyone does constantly and that is crucial to society, both when presented in the guise of formal structures as in legal proceedings and when tossed off in informal groupings.

Metcalf's belief that these humor skills will yield fluidity, creativity, and flexibility makes sense and provides hope.

> I came to understand that emotional responses are like frequencies on a radio dial: if you turn the volume down on one station, you turn it down on all the others at the same time. If you're going to develop joy, laughter, and humor, you will open yourself up to feeling the pain, loss and sadness of the world, too. Or you can opt, as I had done for most of my life, to turn the volume down and never hear the music at all.[4]

As we cope with the cynicism of today's life, his "share, care, dare, and . . . laugh" makes a pretty good mantra for storytellers, clowns, and anyone else who chooses to face life with joy and humor. Most of current humor is quite dark and often quite mean, poking fun at others. Most humor in storytelling is less cruel, although it can contain some harsh jokes. That is one reason I promote old stories, because they remind the hearer that there are other ways of viewing the world than the current one.

In a similar vein is a concern for the earth. We live in such a man-made, artificial environment that it is easy to forget realities that are independent of time, such as the connection between people and between people and the living world, in other words, aspects of life beyond cars and shopping malls. Stories tend to be timeless and connect life as it has always been to current realities in such a way that neither is diminished, and at the same time the hearer is reminded that we are part of a continuum. This means that we have a responsibility to the future and the past as well as the present, which often seems to be the only reality. Few of us think of where food comes from, and being reminded in stories of apple trees and chickens and turnips as part of life rather than as items that require a trip to a supermarket keeps us connected with the joy of life, if only in the abstract.

We are living in a time of great change both in society and in what is considered acceptable within stories. Think about the tale of George Washington cutting down the cherry tree and saying, "I cannot tell a lie." Now, it is ridiculed as a myth. Of course it was, but myths are seen as lies now, rather than their traditional role of symbolic truths that were recognized as parallel to, rather than copying, facts. Truth is being limited to fact in the modern world, and fact is consequently frequently stretched to include what suits the seller/teller. Lying with statistics is legendary. Just try looking at real estate to see what has happened to "truth"—an apartment with a "view of the river" can be on the building's roof, an elevator ride and two staircases away, glimpsed between two distant buildings. As we communicate online, still newer conventions of communication and story are being established. I have had a few students interested in online storytelling, which scares me a little, since it is another distraction from in-person telling, which I consider to be "true storytelling."

My reaction is probably similar to that of people of the nineteenth century who said that canning food is great but eating fresh food is healthier and tastes better. No one listened because having vegetables and fruits in the winter that hadn't been dried was so much better than not having them, and saying anything against it was ridiculous. Well, yes, but anyone who says that a freshly picked spring garden salad is not better than cans of green beans and corn tossed together is either lying or has never enjoyed freshly grown produce. Similarly, although recordings and online storytelling are wonderful—just as written collections are—they cannot match "fresh" telling in person. People are becoming less connected face-to-face, and storytelling is a way of making live connection seem lively and appealing rather than stressful and exhausting. Telling stories is a good way of helping people stay connected and comfortable with each other, in addition to being fun and helping the unconscious mind to grow.

What does all of this "storying around" mean in terms of everyday life and our everyday personal stories? There are set pieces we tell often, others we tell only on particular kinds of occasions, and ones we tell only to ourselves. These are often the most potent—tales about our roles in life, how we have been victimized, our dreams, or whatever else seems important. A sadness of modern society is that we often do not recognize these "self-stories" as stories or consider that they could be consciously edited by the teller (as in therapy) rather than subconsciously shaped out of self-defense. There has been enough attention paid to psychology that we should be more self-aware.

The True Story of the Three Little Pigs by Jon Sciezka provides a perfect example of this self-defense.[5] It is a version of the old folk tale but as told by the wolf, which explains the innocence of his actions.

After all, the sneeze that brought down one pig's house was an accident and in eating the pig that was killed, he was just being a good steward of the environment by not wasting good food. The police arresting him for murder were quite unfair, as he complains and explains from his prison cell. It's too bad he did not become an entertainer—what a waste of a good storyteller of the kind frequently called a "liar." I wonder whether he believes himself?

Usually this kind of story is told inside our heads, where there is a privacy that cannot be invaded, but it is nonetheless often shaped by what others say (or may have said, long ago). We do have the power to construct and revise such stories if we choose to claim that responsibility or are encouraged to revise them by a therapist, but it is not commonly done. Even in times of difficulty or sorrow, there can be pride in survival and in the art of sharing the wisdom gained through an experience, whether it is done consciously as story or not.

According to the Nigerian novelist Ben Okri, "Without stories we would go mad. Life would lose its moorings or lose its orientations. Even in silence we are living our stories."[6]

There is an old joke about men in a prison who had told each other their stories and jokes so many times that they abbreviated them by using numbers. Someone just had to shout out from his cell, "joke 58" and his fellow prisoners would laugh themselves silly as they shared the thought of joke 58. This shared aspect of story is part of what makes it so meaningful.

The shared joy in story is part of the story experience. It is not just the intellectual content that matters but also the sharing of thoughts and the very act of sharing itself. Stories do not have to be funny to be joyful, although that is a good place to start; even sad stories can be joyful if they contain something that transcends the sadness of events and makes them meaningful. You can choose your own example from religious parable, action film, soap opera, or opera libretto, depending on your taste, but the hunger for story is there regardless of one's choice of story forms.

Yes, the hunger for story is there and also the hunger for truth. There was a very interesting discussion on a storytelling listserv a few years ago after Oprah Winfrey expressed her sense of betrayal about James Frey's *A Million Little Pieces*, a book published as a memoir and touted as such although it contained some significant embellishments and fabrications.[7]

Of this, Christopher Maier wrote:

> There are ways of telling personal tales which leave me feeling duped by a teller. I'm not entirely clear exactly when that line gets crossed but my best essay at naming it (today) is to say that I feel duped when I sense a gap between what tellers are telling me and what they know to actually be more true. When they know they are telling a version of reality which at some level is wishful thinking but will sell better.
>
> I certainly concur . . . that truth telling concerns more than just the content of what is said. There are many deeper levels of motivation, aspiration, and what I call consecration that play a role in making for a truthful engagement between teller and listeners. I actually think a teller can tell the exact same content at two different times in their own development and one time it will be far more true for them than another!
>
> I *don't* feel duped if I learn that tellers have condensed several scenes into one or they have invented dialogue that makes explicit what in the actual occurrence may have been largely a nonverbal, energetic exchange. Certainly that's how I read *Angela's Ashes*. . . . I don't believe Frank McCourt transcribed dialogue from a tape recorder he kept with him throughout his harried childhood. Still, I'm grateful he portrayed his childhood with the vividness as if he *had* remembered it that precisely.[8]

Somehow the postmodern world has been messing about with "facts" and "truth" in such a way that they no longer seem as clear as they once were, and the exigencies of publishing make it very tempting to publish something as a memoir even though parts of the story did not happen. Who is the author responsible to? Is it consumers seeking pleasure from reading, publishers seeking profit from the sale of books, some abstract principle about "truth and honesty," or religious or moral beliefs against lying?

So here we are, back again at a variation on the George Washington and the cherry tree issue. What is honest, what is true? Guess what? This is the kind of issue addressed in *stories*. Not just the kind told in sermons with explicit morals attached, but the kind that introduces questions and possible answers and makes the listener think. In other words, the very kind of human fabrication that brought up this issue in the first place.

Storytelling is a way of honoring the traditions that are being brought here by immigrants and teaching those already here about the values of these new cultures in a way that is respectful, not artificial, and enjoyable, not preachy. It is a joy.

One of those joys is knowing that one is connecting children, who are heading into an unknown future, to the past in such a way that our human ancestry will not be completely forgotten. It is exciting to think of connecting to that unknowable past through their tales and their art of storytelling. It is funny to think that those tales were developed (not *written*, but *developed*) at a time when it was assumed that time ran in circles like the seasons, not in the straight line of years today and that change was like the seasons—temporary through the permanence of life—a permanence that had an unknowable but stable transcendence beyond our individual life spans. Religions are based on this perception, as are myths.

There are many reasons why telling stories is important and why it is satisfying, not just for the enjoyment of the occasion but also for civilization in general and for this civilization in a time of major flux. Alfred North Whitehead made a rather scary pronouncement by saying, "The major advances in civilization are processes that all but wreck the societies in which they occur."[9]

Storytelling, as a form of entertainment representing the past and the many ways of being human that are possible, not only can be a joy in itself, but it can also counteract the numbing effect of the enormous changes that we are undergoing in society today. Storytelling not only can prevent wreckage, but it also can make the journey fun for everyone as we travel into this new world we are creating. Tell your stories and have fun.

EXERCISES

Can you define "story"? Is it the same definition you would have given as a child? Is it the same definition you would have given last month?

Think about stories you have heard or read that you had not thought of as "story."

NOTES

1. Arne Nixon was a collector of children's books. There is a special collection at the California State University, Fresno, called the Arne Nixon Center for the Study of Children's Literature.

2. C. W. Metcalf and Roma Felible, *Lighten Up: Survival Skills for People under Pressure* (New York: Addison-Wesley, 1992), 35.

3. Metcalf and Felible, 17.

4. Metcalf and Felible, 39.

5. Jon Scieszka, *The True Story of the Three Little Pigs* (New York: Viking, 1989).

6. Ben Okri, "Aphorisms and Fragments from 'The Joys of Storytelling,'" in *Birds of Heaven* (London: Phoenix, 1996).

7. James Frey, *A Million Little Pieces* (New York: Doubleday, 2004).

8. Christopher Maier, HEALING STORY-L@listserv.american.edu, January 27, 2006.

9. Alfred North Whitehead, *Symbolism: Its Meaning and Effect* (New York: Macmillan, 1927), 88.

Part II

HOW TO BECOME A STORYTELLER

A Living Art

How Does One Learn Stories?
It Is Worth the Effort

These talking machines will ruin the artistic development of music in this country. When I was a boy, in front of every house in the summer evenings, you would find young people together singing the songs of the day or old songs. Today, you hear these infernal machines going night and day. We will not have a vocal chord left in America! The vocal chord will be eliminated by a process of evolution as was the tail of man when he came down from the ape. If you do not make the people executants, you make them depend on the machine.

—John Philip Sousa[1]

History has proved that there is much truth in what Sousa said. When I was young, I was lucky enough to sing in a choir at school and another at church, and I played in an orchestra. When I first got to New York I used to play the recorder in a band with friends. Now I sing rarely and play not at all. And I miss it. How many children take piano lessons today? Now most of us "play" MP3 players with someone else's music that was not even recorded live but required several studio takes with back-up musicians. Most people do not make their own music anymore.

Storytelling is also in danger. It should not be—although not everyone is lucky enough to have music lessons—we all learn to talk. So anyone can tell stories, and even those who don't tell can listen. The point is that there is a live human connection that is not there with movies, recordings, or online, as appealing and wonderful as they are.

This is a great gift to be able to give anyone. And it can be an important gift. When asked why he told stories, Brother Blue, a famous storyteller and the official storyteller of Boston and Cambridge, once said, "I tell stories to keep people from committing suicide."[2] Blue's statement may be a little melodramatic, but stories can offer real support in facing genuine problems. Few of us will prevent a suicide, but we may well make life a little more pleasant or understandable for those who listen to our stories. Listening is much deeper than reading. We have only been reading for a few centuries, but we have talked and told stories for millennia. It is well worth the effort to learn the art.

They say that what is taken in by the ear is taken in with emotion, while what is taken in by the eye is taken in with automatic acceptance rather than thought, because in the natural world it is harder to "lie" visually—if you see a bear you get out of there. This is not the place for philosophical discussions about modern society and its dependency on visual media like television, but one of the reasons I push for storytelling that sets up readers to create their own illustrations in their minds and learn how to think and imagine freely.

Some say that this is easier to do in a group, that minds simultaneously work both together and individually in groups. Whether that is true or not, people find it fun to do. And learning the story you are listening to used to be automatic. Now most of us have to make an effort to learn tales, even those that have been heard before; even harder is learning from books, an art that today's storytellers must learn.

Most people who are not born storytellers find the subject of how to learn a story frightening. It does not need to be. For years I have been teaching storytelling in a one-week format, and by Friday morning everyone has been able to tell at least one folk tale they have learned. They have also told stories about their own life or their family's and tales they learned elsewhere—in bed as a child from their grandma or grandpa or from a teacher or a friend. It could have been from a mean person trying to scare them, a frightened person trying to share their own fear, or perhaps from a wise person or religious teacher trying to share a point to be understood.

We are concerned at the moment with telling traditional tales, like folk tales, religious stories from Biblical and other religious traditions, as well as other stories from historical sources. You must select a story for the audience, but it is wise to have a few in reserve in case the audience is not what you expected. Crafting a tellable story out of personal experience is a related but a different art. Right now we are concerned with learning a traditional story.

The primary task, of course, is to choose a story. It might make more sense on the face of it to discuss choosing a story to learn first, but experience suggests that thinking about how you are going to approach learning a story may affect your choices. Choosing a story is covered soon. If you are impatient, feel free to go on to chapter 6 and come back to this chapter later.

So, how does one learn a story? When I started learning, as a librarian and student, the rule was that you memorized, word for word. Period. If you can do that from written material, as actors do, that is wonderful, and you are a very lucky person. Some people automatically remember what they have read. This kind of eidetic memory is not uncommon, and I have known a few friends and students who have it. Most of us, however, do not have such an ability and must work at it. Just suck it up and accept that this is work. Not all stories need to be memorized word for word, but let's start the discussion with memorizing.

Some people find that copying a story from a book helps them to learn it. The very act of having the words go through your eyes into your brain and then out your fingers helps you learn it. Unfortunately, unlike theater, there are no lines from other characters to act as prompts, so dividing it into small sections can make it more manageable. Just be sure to break it into logical sections, maybe scenes or character descriptions, rather than simple page breaks.

Some people find that reading it aloud into a recording device and then playing that reading again and again helps them to learn it. Those people who commute long distances in their cars can use this method to good advantage. Instead of listening to the radio, learn a new story. Others find that listening to a story while in bed preparing to sleep works well. It allows the unconscious to work overnight.

The only warning I have in regard to this method is to realize the danger of memorization. The story can become dead or zombie-like if one memorizes it not from life but a recording.

Elizabeth Ellis tells of her son, Scooter, who happened to go to a shopping center and heard a woman telling one of Elizabeth's stories in the first person: about "my son" and "I." As it happens, it was a very difficult story, about something very painful that had happened to Scooter and that had required some careful negotiating between them before he allowed Elizabeth to tell his story in public. And here was this person "lying" by telling it in the first person as if she were Scooter's mother. Now, Scooter had already gotten used to the weird world of storytellers out of plain old self-defense, but this was too much and he bawled out the storyteller in public.

Clearly this person had memorized from the recording, and it was a personal story about something that had happened to Scooter; it was not a folk tale from an anonymous teller. This was zombie-like, if not outright theft, taking on someone else's life and claiming what happened to that person as if it happened to you. The same is true of one's storytelling style; one can adapt but should not slavishly adopt someone else's style. In terms of content, a certain amount of freedom with reality is expected among storytellers, but either one tells it in such a way that indicates that it is clearly made up or adopted or one says something in the introduction or conclusion to the story about its source. Integrity is required, because listeners, particularly children, want to know if something is "true," and they will ask if a story is true, something we will talk about elsewhere.

Originally, I was using the term "zombie-like" to refer to rote memorization, which dooms one to telling in a rote way, but there is also another concern. Many of us read in an unreal or "dead voice," and learning from such a recording is setting oneself up for a less-than-ideal performance. Sometimes getting a friend (or two or three) to read the story aloud helps one to learn it in a more natural way. The temptation to learn from a good storyteller is understandable, but know that it can be dangerous and should only be one avenue for learning about tales and how to tell them.

There are many storytellers now with Web sites that offer sample stories. If you don't have experience listening to live storytellers, listen to some of these and compare their styles. Theatrical? Sly? Buffoon? Be sure to listen to several rather than just a few, and don't pattern yourself by copying someone else. Better yet, go to a storytelling festival and get caught up in the shared audience experience. Many states and local areas have such festivals. Remember to try fresh peas, not just canned or frozen.

There are many styles that will fit you, and they may change over time. My only advice is this: it is much better to start with a straightforward style and later experiment with more mannered styles than to begin with a clownish or pompous style. It is much more difficult to let mannerisms go than it is to add them experimentally when you are already comfortable with a straight style that you can return to if the experiment is not successful. Do you know *The Peterkin Papers* by Elizabeth Hale? She tells a story about accidentally putting salt in coffee. The Peterkin family offers advice on what to add to the coffee to remove the flavor of salt, but it is only when the "Lady from Philadelphia" suggests making a fresh cup of coffee that a decent flavor results.[3]

Now, both the methods described—memorizing from written versions and memorizing from a recorded telling—are ways of learning an exact reproduction. When I began storytelling for the library world, this was the only acceptable way of doing it. That is still true if one wants to learn an *original story* that was written by an author, such as Hans Christian Andersen or Carl Sandburg. It is also true if one is learning some myths or other tales in which the language is a crucial part of the story. Most stories, however, do not need word-for-word memorization, so we will discuss several alternate methods so that you will present a story you "know" and tell, not one you have slavishly memorized and recite like an automaton. Some tellers do better one way and some another; there is no one right way to learn all stories.

There are also methods that primarily use one or more of the senses: eye in terms of memorizing from text and ear in terms of learning from listening. Because stories are primarily heard in a performance, hearing makes particular sense as a way to learn, but we all have our own methods.

There are other tricks that people with various types of learning styles can use. Many people have found that drawing sketches of scenes works (and no, artistic skill is not a requirement—poor quality cartoon-style sketches work fine). You can use a storyboard notebook with frames for pictures and space underneath for lines. If you wanted to use this, for example, with "The Three Bears," the first scene you might draw would be a cottage with a big bear, a medium-sized bear, and a tiny bear standing in front of it. Then an interior "shot" with the bears getting out of big, medium-sized, and tiny beds. Then the three bears in their chairs.

Then Mama Bear making porridge and serving it in three bowls with the stove at one end of the cottage and the table at the other, and Father and Baby bear waiting as Mama walks from the stove with motion lines behind her. Then a picture of them leaving for their walk.

Then a picture of the cottage by itself with Goldilocks trying the door.

Then another with Goldilocks sitting in the chairs with "motion lines" from one chair to another, and then a picture of the third chair broken with Goldilocks on the floor.

Then trying the porridge. Maybe another picture, with steam from one, ice cubes over the other, and a smile over the third.

Then trying the three beds and curling up on the third, again, with motion lines between them.

Finally, the dénouement: the three bears returning to the cottage and waking Goldilocks, who runs out.

If you want, you can satisfy yourself at the end with a picture of the three bears cleaning up the cottage and having their porridge, and another of Goldilocks still running or maybe safe at home. You would not include these in a telling ordinarily, but it might make it easier for you to smile at the end, as you connect with the audience as yourself again.

Obviously, one can develop a system of symbols that work well for the person using it. As someone who is not very visual and who cannot draw, this is something I seldom use for myself, but I know several people who swear by it. Apparently visualizing these pictures can lower fears about forgetting something and can distract from performance anxiety. Stick figures, representing the characters in the story; a tree representing the scene's setting in a forest or a wave to show it is on the beach; crossed swords or a circle around a cross to indicate that it is a scene of conflict or a love scene—all of these can be visualized while telling to cue the teller who has a visual memory.

Another system some people use is choosing a room that one knows well and, in your mind, going from corner to wall to next corner, and so forth, connecting a scene with each picture, chair, mirror, and so on. Again, this has the benefit of associating something familiar and comforting with the story. Many people find it reassuring to use something familiar that you feel safe about remembering. A variant of this method is to associate the story's scenes with some set of symbols that are important to you. You can use the letters of the alphabet or a breakdown of letters and numbers as one does in an academic paper outline with Roman numerals, capital letters, Arabic numerals, and lowercase letters. In other words, you are making an outline of the story. Remembering details will happen, even if you don't include them in the outline. Just make sure that you include everything that is needed to understand the story. This works for some but may be too detached for others. If so, try using the names of your favorite sports team or ballet corps, the names of the streets from your house to that of someone you are in love with, or whatever you feel comfortable with remembering and can put it in a mnemonic sequence.

It is interesting that listening to a story told will often lock it in your mind almost automatically. Something that I have often asked students in class to do is to go out and tell a simple story they just heard me tell. They are asked to tell it at least three times, preferably to three different people, but pets and family members can hear it more than once. We are wired to be able to retell something that we just heard but few of us have developed this ability, and psychologists tell us that it is something that must be practiced from childhood. Even so, most of us can repeat a simple story if we do it fairly soon after hearing it, and once it has been told three times, it becomes ours to tell for a long time.

Regardless of how you learn it, however, know that it is possible to forget stories. There are many I regret having forgotten as times change and audiences change along with them. It is much easier to relearn a story from a recording of your own voice, so after making the effort of learning a story, it is a good idea to record it to help jog your memory. In the past, I did not do this, and I have forgotten several stories that I once told and find myself attracted to again, years later. It will take months of work to reshape them from printed sources and then relearn and remember them, instead of reclaiming them in a few days by listening to them.

The next chapter is about choosing a story to tell, but I want to end this chapter with the idea that the effort is worth it. Whether you are someone who can listen just once and retell a story or someone who has to work at it, it is worth the effort. This is what Duncan Williamson, who grew up as a Traveler,[4] has to say about his people, one of the few groups that had a strong oral tradition in Britain in the twentieth century:

> Storytelling in traveler society is not just meant for children. When I was twenty-four years of age, a grown man with three children, I sat with my brother and my cousins from ten o'clock one night until six o'clock in the morning listening to an old man telling us tales. We spent a full night listening to him and never noticed the time passing. He knew something about everything: he told us tales of the war, stories of his past, from his boyhood days, things he had heard sixty years before from his own family. He told how things were free and easy in his day, what it was to be happy and free. And we had a feeling of peace and freedom. We were just like Indians sitting on a mountain top—no cares in the world, we had nothing—just a voice from this old man whom we respected so much. He told us so many things, things of life that stood us in good stead through our entire days. I would give all the money in the world to go back right now to that night, the only difference would be, I would sit longer. Until the day that I die and leave this world I will remember him. And he knew in his own mind that he was telling us something that would be remembered years after he was gone. That was the way with all travelers.
>
> It's not just the story. It is something to last a person for his entire life, something that's been passed down from tradition: that's what stories mean to the travelling people. They know their children are going out in the world, and some day they will be gone. The children need something to remember their forbears by, not monuments in graveyards or marble stones. The travelling people know they are giving their children something far better: mothers and fathers know if their children follow the stories they hear at the fireside, and live accordingly, then they cannot help but remember who taught them stories. Travellers give you the tale so *they* will never be forgotten.[5]

This hunger for old stories is still true. I was complaining about the fact that more and more of what is available on Broadway is rehashed movies when it used to be the other way around, with *South Pacific*, *Oklahoma*, and other such blockbuster Broadway shows being turned into movies. A friend who works on Broadway calmly replied that it was the appeal of the known story we have just been discussing. Now the bulk of attendees at Broadway shows are tourists, and they want the familiar. Perhaps New York is overstimulating enough in itself, but I choose to believe that the impulse to see such shows comes from the fact that even in the current world, there is a hunger for "old" stories. It is a human condition, even in our overstimulated, sensation-hungry twenty-first-century world. You are needed as a storyteller, wherever you choose to tell—on the front porch, in the kitchen, in Sunday School, in a classroom, or, if you turn out to be a brilliant star, in a huge tent in Jonesboro at the National Storytelling Festival.

EXERCISES

In the meantime, try these patterns of learning with a story you just heard in class or on a recording. If you are on your own, you might listen to a recording or choose one of Margie MacDonald's easy-to-learn stories in *The Storyteller's Start-up Book* or *Twenty Tellable Tales*.[6] Or you can start with something easy to learn, perhaps a short nursery tale you already are familiar with, like "The Gingerbread Boy" or "Three Billy Goats Gruff."

If you want to get started learning a story right now, you might pick one story—modern, classic, Shakespearian, or traditional—and see how many versions you can find. For example, consider Frankenstein. There is Mary Shelley's novel, the film versions, including Mel Brooks's *Young Frankenstein*, and several picture book and manga versions, as well as old Jewish golem folk tales. Think about why this story's appeal is so strong that it has been worth telling in so many ways.

More importantly, find two or three stories that speak to you and at least three or four versions of each in order to decide which you would consider telling. Warning: it could be that you will find the same version of a story in several books—all copied from Grimm. You might be lucky, though, with a story as popular as "Cinderella," you might find a number of versions: "Cendrillon" in the Perrault version, a straight Grimm "Ashchenputtel," which is quite different, and the Wanda Gag retelling. For the moment, ignore modern retellings set in other locations. Just know that there are whole books (and dissertations) devoted to variants of Cinderella, from ancient Egypt to modern New Orleans. Have fun rummaging.

NOTES

1. This quote from Sousa was from a congressional hearing in 1906. Posted by DJA on 16 December 16, 2008, http://secretsociety.typepad.com/ darcy_james_argues_secret/2008/10/infernal-machine.html (accessed January 11, 2010). A slightly different version is available at http://en.wikipedia.org/ wiki/John_Philip_Sousa (accessed January 10, 2010).

2. Dan Yashinsky, *Suddenly They Heard Footsteps: Storytelling for the Twenty-first Century* (Jackson: University Press of Mississippi, 2004), 173.

3. Elizabeth Hale, *The Peterkin Papers* (Boston: Houghton Mifflin, 1880). It is available online through Project Gutenberg.

4. The term "gypsy" is viewed as an insult. Romani is also acceptable.

5. Duncan Williamson, *Fireside Tales of the Traveller Children: Twelve Scottish Stories* (Edinburgh: Harmony Books, 1985), xvii.

6. Margaret Read MacDonald, *The Storyteller's Start-up Book: Finding, Learning, Performing, and Using Folktales: Including Twelve Tellable Tales* (Little Rock, AR: August House, 1993) and *Twenty Tellable Tales: Audience Participation Folktales for the Beginning Storyteller* (New York: H. W. Wilson, 1986).

CHAPTER 5

Types of Stories

Tradition is the handing on of fire and not the worship of ashes.

—Gustav Mahler

Choosing a story to tell is very important, so an overview is a good place to start. What culture told it? Was it for a special occasion? Is it funny or serious? All of these are helpful to know. You will find a category that suits you—maybe a culture that a grandmother came from so that you feel connected to it—maybe an audience that you enjoy working with, be it businessmen or kindergartners. It could be that you enjoy telling tall tales—"lying" without hurting anyone, just for the fun of it. Maybe you want to offer support for people going through some type of loss or pain. All of these are good categories and only a small sample of potential types of stories and audiences. Think of going to a supermarket. Are you attracted to fruits, fish, or baked goods, or do you want some of each? It depends on who you are and what your plans are.

It is clear that the first issue in storytelling is what story to tell, so let's go "shopping." There are many types of stories, and one can easily become confused by the distinctions among them. Some types, for example, refer to the story's origins, while others are about the style of story. Remember, stories go back to the beginnings of human culture, when science and scholarship did not exist, so don't expect neat categories and straight lines.

This system, described below, was developed by library storytellers and catalogers for organizing them. It is similar to the anthropological distinctions, but from a teller's perspective rather than that of a scientist.

The easiest way to begin is to explain the different categories and discuss the implications of these distinctions for those looking for tales to tell.

Folklore is the generic name for all kinds of folk stories, jokes, and superstitions. In library tradition, folk and fairy tales were shelved together. In spite of the name, fairy tales do not have to be stories about fairies. They were written by modern authors in folk tale idiom. Since they were read by readers of folk tales, it made sense that they should be kept with the folk tales. In the Dewey system, folk literature and fiction were shelved separately. So children's librarians figured out this way of keeping similar books together, in folk and fairy tale collections, without getting into fights with catalogers over cheating on the principle of separating fiction and nonfiction. Children's libraries are still an excellent place to begin research on stories for telling because they have such good collections of folklore and fairy tales of all kinds.

Let's begin with what libraries call *fairy tales*. These include the stories of Rudyard Kipling, Carl Sandburg, Hans Christian Andersen, and many others. Such stories are the work of a particular mind and deserve to be memorized and repeated just as they were intended. The only way I can emphasize this enough is to say that they should be treated like the Bible. Scholars may compare Biblical versions and argue about them, but the ordinary person is expected to accept it as gospel and not mess with it. Creativity is, according to some experts, currently being lost; whether or not this is true, it should be respected where it exists and not "messed with," regardless of copyright laws. People may get away with rewriting Hans Christian Andersen tales under their own names, but it is wrong. Again, this is an issue of integrity as well as copyright.

Folk tales are those stories that have been told through many generations for so long that no one knows who originally thought them up, who changed them, or how. They represent the values of the culture that they come from. In most European cultures, these included kindness, steadfastness, bravery, and honesty. Honesty is, I hope, self-evident in its value, for it invokes trust and similar honesty on the part of others. Steadfastness was often represented by the hero taking three tries at most tasks and succeeding on the third try. Bravery usually takes the form of fighting evil, risking danger, or some other test, usually for the benefit of someone else. Kindness was evident in the many stories of a third son or daughter sharing their last bit of food with someone even hungrier than they are. Often it was this pathetic figure with whom the third child shared their food who in turn shared the wisdom that helped the hero or heroine solve the problem of the story. Older brothers or sisters were sometimes too self-important to listen to anyone unimportant, so they missed the wisdom.

Wonder tales are a cross between fairy tales and myths. They are usually literary versions of tales that were originally myths.

Pourquoi tales are tales that explain why something is the way it is, as the French word suggests. They can be myths or folktales or urban legends. One story on the Wilson videotapes tells of a storytelling occasion when, on a long walk, the explanation of why trees let their leaves fall in autumn was told by both a traditional tribal teller and also by someone with a scientific perspective.[1] Each claimed to be truth, with the tribal elder pointing out the cleverness of the tribal deity for figuring out how to make his explanation come about through using the scientific explanation. To the storyteller, this is a great vignette, for it shows how the storyteller can incorporate what others would see as proof of the story being false.

Myths should be treated with respect, for *myths* were once believed as part of a religious system. Once again, whether myths are part of your belief system or not, they deserve to be treated with respect. That means, do not tell them to ridicule what others once believed, but it also means recognizing that the story can be interpreted on different levels and should not be reshaped or retold to suit your personal fancy. For example, Native American stories tend to involve four attempts at resolving a problem, following the honoring of the four directions. Shortening it to three, in order to suit European taste, is not appropriate.

There are other bits of anthropological etiquette that should be understood, as well. There are cultures, such as those of the Pacific Northwest, in which stories are personal property. If a story is revealed to you during a time of isolation or meditation, it is your story. You might will it to someone by telling that person that he or she has the right to tell it upon your death, but otherwise that story is lost once you cease telling it, and it is completely gone when those who have heard it forget it or die. The idea may be shocking to current ears, which are used to private information being thrown around on the news and recycled from one version to another, but it is worth thinking about.

Another point of storytelling etiquette is when one can tell a story. Even today we recognize that a story told on a stag night is inappropriate for a tea party or for an audience of children. Some cultures have times for stories in general or for particular stories. Several Native American tribes have specific traditions regarding this. In the summer and fall, you should be outside hunting meat to be dried for winter. Wintertime, when one could be trapped inside a tepee for days at a time, perhaps with limited food, was a good time for going inside one's own mind and quietly reflecting. This was a good time for what was sometimes called winter-telling tales, which were mythic tales that made one think about the meaning of life.

Legends supposedly happened. Many have a religious base, but even those that don't usually have a lesson, whether overtly stated or not. For example, there is a famous legend about someone who hears of a hidden fortune that he will be able to find by following the instructions of a dream. He does so only to discover that the fortune is right back where he started but hidden.[2] Usually he learns of it from someone else who is scornful of dreams and such foolishness. There are many versions of this tale from Europe and the Middle East. I know of at least four. It is like a Sufi tale about learning how to follow one's own inner voice to find truth. Myths and legends are often grouped together.

Fables are stories that have a lesson, and animals are usually the main characters. Aesop's fables are the best known in the European/American tradition, and those of Reynard the Fox are still very much a part of French literature, while those of Anansi the Spider are still told both in Africa and the Caribbean, and Brer Rabbit tales are loved in the American South.

Parables are teaching stories, usually with a strong moral attached, whether or not it is specifically stated. Both Christ and Buddha are famous for the parables they told. Sufi stories are a kind of parable, but often the moral is something that requires serious pondering, like those of Zen stories.

Ballads can be any kind of story, although they are usually romantic. What makes them ballads is that they are songs. Very often now we only have them in printed form, which looks like poetry, but ideally they should be sung, not read.

Hero tales are self-explanatory. They are about heroes and heroines who go on quests to try to right a wrong or find an answer. These are about courage and bravery and steadfastness. The modern stories about Superman fit the mold very clearly, as does Star Wars' Luke Skywalker.

Epics tend to be cycles of stories about heroes. Often they are constellations of stories, some of which contradict each other. Think of King Arthur and the conflicting accounts of what happened between him and Guinevere and when—or if—he will return.

Modern fantasy can take on epic issues and become a kind of epic. *The Lord of the Rings* is a good example, for it uses much folkloric material and deals with the same issues of good and evil and of power and its temptations. *Medieval romances* were the equivalent in their day. These tales were romantic in the sense of dealing with Sturm und Drang, rather than the modern sense of romance dealing just with love.

Drolls are silly stories meant to be taken as jokes. Japanese tradition used these to warm up the audience before telling longer, more serious tales.

Tall tales are primarily an American specialty, with Paul Bunyan and John Henry probably being the best known. Perhaps the work camps of men who had nothing to read and who were largely illiterate were good breeding grounds for liars. There are other traditions, also, like the European Baron Munchausen stories. *Tall tales* were wildly exaggerated stories that were supposed to be taken as jokes as much as stories, but with elements of truth in them.

Urban legends are, in a way, the modern equivalent of tall tales, and anyone who has not tripped over Snopes.com is recommended to look there. You may find something that you believed to be true there.

Very often stories deal with issues present in people's minds. For example, there is that old story about the "hook": a boy and girl are "parking" in the forest when they hear a story on the radio about an escaped madman with a hook for a hand. They hear a strange noise outside and take off, only to find a hook, à la Captain Hook, stuck in the car's door handle when they get home.

This legend originated when cars were new in society and young people were alone together in ways that had not been possible before. Sexual mores were changing and this caused some anxiety on the part of young couples that wanted to be good but also felt temptation under circumstances that did not prevent them from acting upon those desires.

A student of mine recently told me about a friend of her daughter's, who took her pet boa constrictor to the vet because he had stopped eating.

The snake slept in her bed, and they had become close, so she was truly worried. The vet told her that the snake had stopped eating mice because he was preparing to eat her.

Now, I don't know if this really happened or not. It was not on Snopes.com when I looked, and my student believed it. Someone showed me pictures on the Internet of a snake that had swallowed someone. I don't wish to be cruel to someone who may have been in real emotional pain after being told this about an animal she loved, but it says something about our current need to stay in touch with the natural world. You can decide whether this is a "true" story or an urban legend, but either way there is a lesson in it.

The Darwin Awards are also a kind of tribute to storytelling and modern life. They are awarded posthumously to people who have died in the most ridiculous ways. One person, for example, attached jet engines to a car that crashed when it went over a hill out-of-control. They are mean but also funny. These are the equivalent of modern legends.

However, we are getting distracted by stories. The topic at hand is that of the different kinds of tales. The urban legend is the kind of tale that tends to be told around a campfire rather than in formal performances. If that is your kind of storytelling, have fun.

One of the best kinds of stories to listen to is the *personal story*. I used to listen to an acquaintance who had been a mountain climbing guide tell the most incredible stories based on his experiences. His ability to tell of terrible dangers and suspenseful rescues was amazing, and I used to wonder if telling stories had been part of what made him successful as a guide, keeping up hope in times of trouble.

Another amazing storyteller I ran into was someone on a train trip across the Canadian prairie. He was probably a pathological liar, but who cares? His stories of escaping from East Germany by literally "going *out* through the *in* door" at a railway station and volunteering at an embassy to be a spy were wonderful. This kind of storytelling is referred to as the *raconteur* tradition. They are usually stories told by the person who supposedly experienced them, and they require imagination as well as telling skill.

Traditional *folk tales* come from unknown tellers and have been told by many people over time. Some can be traced through time and place, but even so, the individuals who originated them are unknown.

Sometimes these tales have been retold by individuals who have put their name on them. This goes back to people like Charles Perrault, who retold French tales, and Mme. de Beaumont who told new stories with folk themes. It is also true of the Brothers Grimm who tried to be faithful to the stories as they were told by the "folk"—usually illiterate peasants telling tales that they had learned at their mother's knee (or uncle's or neighbor's). The Grimms had Victorian sensibilities and changed a few stories by cleaning them up, but by and large they remain as told.

You will trip over all these terms in books about stories and telling, so be prepared and don't get overwhelmed by all the distinctions—just know that there are many types of stories and that some will be suitable for you to tell. You may find that tales from one tradition or another appeal to you, or it may be that one type of story works best for you regardless of where it comes from. The point is that you must approach them all with respect and research the background so that you treat it appropriately and introduce it to your audience in a way that makes sense and is respectful. You do not have to be a certified folklorist, just know enough to make sensible choices for yourself and your audience.

If you find a particular tradition that attracts you, and you are telling to mostly adult audiences, then look in adult collections for more sophisticated tales.

Either way, once you have your sea legs and want to research further, you need to become familiar with Stith Thompson's *Motif-index of Folk Literature*.[3] This is an anthropological tool that approaches stories from different perspectives, mostly in terms of content. It is difficult to become comfortable with, but it is very useful. However, it does not include recent collections, but only older titles, most of which are still available. It remains the standard and is available now online, but is still difficult to navigate.[4] There have been updates and several more recent attempts to organize an approach to finding stories. Margaret Read MacDonald has done this particularly well, having experience in both storytelling and the anthropological study of folklore. Her indexes are much easier to use.[5]

If you find all this fascinating, good, but you may find it overwhelming and not want to start with research at this point, thank you very much! That's fine too. Remember this is an art that precedes books and scholars. If you just want to know some good stories to start with, look in the Storiography in appendix A of this book. If you can wait, the next chapter discusses choosing appropriate stories for specific audiences.

EXERCISES

Think about stories you know—or even books or movies—and the categories they might fit into. It is interesting to see how often modern tales follow old patterns.
    Select a few stories from each category to see if you understand the distinctions.

NOTES

1. Ron Evans, *Why the Leaves Change Color*, American Storytelling Series, vol. 7 (New York: Wilson Video Resource Collection, 1986). Ron is a "Keeper of Talking Sticks" for the Chippewa Cree of Alberta.

2. This is available in an old English version from Elizabeth Ellis, "Peddlar of Swaffham," American Storytelling Series, vol. 2 (New York: Wilson Video Resource Collection, 1986). A stone memorializes the event in Swaffham. A picture book of the Jewish version is available from Uri Shulevitz, *The Treasure* (New York: Farrar, Straus and Giroux, 1978).

3. Stith Thompson, *Motif-index of Folk-literature: A Classification of Narrative Elements in Folktales, Ballads, Myths, Fables, Mediaeval Romances, Exempla, Fabliaux, Jest-books, and Local Legends* (Bloomington: Indiana University Press, 1955–1958).

4. Stith Thompson, *Motif index of Folk Literature*, www.ruthenia.ru/folklore/thompson/g.html (accessed January 19, 2010).

5. Margaret Read MacDonald, *The Storyteller's Sourcebook: A Subject, Title, and Motif-index to Children's Folklore Collections* (Farmington Mills, MI: Gale, 1982). See also Margaret Read MacDonald and Brian Sturm, *The Storyteller's Sourcebook: A Subject, Title, and Motif-index to Children's Folklore Collections, 1983–1999* (Farmington Mills, MI: Gale, 2002).

CHAPTER 6

Selecting a Story, and Version, to Tell

> Storytellers must also be story listeners. Finding a story is the first step. Then the story should be studied and connected to its roots, whether an author, a culture or a folk tradition. Proper storytelling etiquette requires giving credit to sources and respecting copyrights. Gradually the story takes on a personal meaning within. Then the storyteller begins to tell it as his or her own.
>
> —Barry McWilliams[1]

This chapter is about selecting stories in a good version for you to tell. As we discussed earlier, individuals have distinct styles of telling, so different tellers find different types of stories and different versions of the same stories appropriate. One may like dry witty humor, for instance, and another prefer slapstick. Both tellers could do either version, but one fits better. There is a Storiography included at the end of this book to help you find stories that have been proven with recent audiences.

Each of us is individual, and each of us has many facets. One may enjoy flirting and have a "true-to-one-mate" heart; another may be a great flirt and enjoy continuing to the logical conclusion. A third person may repress such desire, and a fourth may not even feel pleasure in talking to another person, let alone flirting. Each is a valid way of being, just different.

One may seek truth and another may find such search for truth to be self-important claptrap. The story you choose to tell should suit your own sense of values, sense of humor, and comfort level with self-exposure. When I began, I told silly stories so I could join in the laughter without worrying about people laughing at me. On the other hand, many say that humorous stories are tough to begin with, because if people don't laugh you are in big trouble. Angela Lansbury has said that she could not sing a song before an audience as herself, ever, but she could easily sing as a character without any trouble.[2] That makes sense to me, for in one case you are risking yourself as a singer; in the other it is someone else you are "playing," who may or may not be able to sing well, so your ego is not involved.

Look at this another way. People can go skating at a skating rink just for the fun of it, or they can be figure skaters, hockey players, distance skaters, or speed skaters. They can do it professionally or for enjoyment or take lessons or give them. People can also skate not only at skating rinks, but on ponds or lakes or rivers and wear old strap-on skates like Hans Brinker or figure skates. All are skaters. Likewise, storytellers come in all shapes and sizes and tell at bedtime, on bus trips, and in bars, as well as in more formal settings. Different stories and styles of stories are appropriate for different occasions.

All these approaches are valid. All are fun, for teller and hearer both. None are wrong, just different. Find what works for you. An in-person teacher can make suggestions, but the truth is you must figure it out for yourself, whether you have a teacher or not. It cannot be given to you, it must be figured out.

But the topic is choosing tales. So, after deciding who you are as a beginning storyteller and what style of telling suits you, you must find a story that you like. There will be a lot of time spent with a story you prepare to tell for an audience, so it is, if not like a marriage, at least like choosing an apartment that one can live in. Yes, it is possible to move, but breaking a lease can be expensive. So put some effort in at the beginning. In terms of storytelling, that means investing the time in finding a story you like and, equally important, a version that you like. Believe me, it is worth it to invest this effort early on.

One of the important points to consider is your own background and heritage. Don't use an accent unless it is comfortable for you. It is enough to remember the story and stay connected with the audience without trying to remain true to a fake accent. On the other hand, you do not necessarily need to be born to a style in order to use it.

I grew up in Vancouver at a time when there were many immigrants from Scotland, so I learned about "jilly baigs" (a bag for making jelly) and sporrans (the metal and fur decoration that hangs in front of a kilt), ate haggis (the "delicacy" of oats, sheep's stomach, and other organs) served on Robbie Burns night with gravy, and I adored going to military tattoos (no, not skin decorations, but band concerts with marching and bagpipes). One day when I was in seventh grade, a friend who was a recent arrival from Ireland and I made a phone call to another friend. At the time, there were still phone operators in Vancouver, and when I heard "number please," I answered with the number. It was not until I saw the look on my friend's face that I realized that I had given the number in a good Glaswegian accent, mirroring the phone operator's accent. My friend didn't know if I was making fun of her Irish accent—and doing it badly—or what. It was completely unconscious on my part, like a child responding to one language at home and another in the street or at school.

There are two points here: First is a demonstration of the fact that if you need to include explanations, as in the previous paragraph, you will probably lose most of your audience. Interruptions are a dangerous risk. Second is that you should only use an accent if it truly feels natural.

If an accent does not feel natural, don't use it. You risk offending people in the audience who feel that they are being mocked and irritating others who sense that it is wrong. (Have you ever watched a British show with an actor pretending to be American who sounds not like an American but like a British actor trying to be an American?) It is okay to include one or two signature words with an accent but be careful.

This issue of language is something to think about. We speak elsewhere about negotiating between your own love of words and unsophisticated listeners, but this is important in this context, also. You are telling stories to an audience, not just to a mirror, so you have to think of that audience. One of the nicest aspects of storytelling is that it can fit any group. It can be classless and ageless or carefully targeted to a specific group. Most stories have an anthropological background, and they can be used to introduce the values and language of one culture to another, but many have a broad appeal with elements that appeal to one group or another. For example, younger children love repetition, while older children demand that justice be done and villains be properly punished. Meanwhile, teenagers and adults hunger for meaning, and almost everyone wants a satisfying ending and beautiful language. That last should not be misinterpreted—girls want pretty language, while strong and stark words appeal to boys. The point is that the words must fit the story. Telling of murders in pretty language, describing the beauty of blood pouring over alabaster skin and the pride filling the heart of a killer is not ordinarily appropriate.

The point is that there are stories, and versions of the same story, that fit almost any teller and any audience. The artistry lies in finding and choosing stories and versions of those stories that fit both. Elsewhere we mentioned *The True Story of the Three Little Pigs*, where the story is told from the wolf's point of view.[3] That is a picture book, and delightful, but it should not be used with children who do not know the original story and definitely not with young children who do not yet understand sarcasm and irony.

Just as one would not tell jokes about sex to young children, Greek tragedies do not belong in such a setting, either. It is worth doing a little work in selecting not only the story, but also the version you choose to spend hours and weeks learning.

This might be a good place to say that it is important to understand the difference between written and spoken language. Sometimes the best versions to curl up with are not the best for telling. Beginning speechwriters have to learn this and storytellers do, also. Sometimes written language doesn't just sound pompous, it sounds unreal. That doesn't mean it can't be correct formal language, but it has to be the language of speech, not of written literature. I don't know how else to describe it, but try reading it to someone or tape it and listen. It can feel unreal but not fake. You will develop your own ear for what you can tell well.

Another even more serious issue is being careful about the stories you choose to tell. Obvious is the respect one must feel for stories of other cultures. That includes content and other issues. Many cultures have serious restrictions on stories. For example, as is discussed earlier, many Native American traditions tell stories only in the winter. In the summer, you are supposed to be outside, spending your time preparing for winter by hunting and gathering. In the winter, forced inside by bad weather, one has time to let the imagination roam and prevent feeling too limited by the cold. Other cultures, again including some Native American ones, have personal stories that are literally a kind of property—perhaps because it was developed (or experienced) as a deeply felt spiritual experience or perhaps just an imaginative tale, but either way, the story dies out, except in the memory of the person who has heard it, unless the owner of the story gives someone else the right to tell it before he or she dies. This is a form of "honor copyright," just as American culture used to honor one's word with a handshake. Know what you are getting into. Just as someone might be offended by a person who told a Bible story and made fun of it, show respect for a story and its tradition. If you can't, don't tell that story.

In some cultures, stories were told by bards trained in memorizing the legends of their culture. The *seanachie*[4] of the Celtic tradition went to the villages to tell stories imbued with the values of the tradition; they were a form of priest carrying the sacred stories. I was lucky enough to hear Padraic Colum tell, and he was literally mesmerizing. I always think of his performance when I think of a *seanachie*.

I have had students who felt they had the right to rewrite stories. One was offended by the idea of a girl sacrificing her life for the bell her father was making. Filial piety, even unto death, is a respected part of Chinese culture. I told her she could not rewrite the story or delete that part without destroying the story and that she should choose another story. Someone else wanted to use a Hindu story for a Catholic Sunday School and planned to turn deities into angels.

Again, don't mess with other people's religions; even ones that are no longer practiced deserve respect. I have one friend who followed his ancient Icelandic traditions, worshiping Thor and Odin, another who is Parsi, and have even had a couple of students identify themselves as Wiccan, so you can't make a blanket statement like "no one follows such old religions." Give the same respect you would want for your own religion.

As my students know, I am very much against learning stories in the abstract without finding out about the surrounding culture. It is important to know that Iktomi/Spider, Raven, Loki, and other tricksters play important roles in their societies, bringing change and being mistrusted because of it. If you are fond of such stories, be sure to research the culture so that you can understand and project that role in your telling, not in a lecture. You do not have to become an anthropologist, but at least find out some basic information about the culture's values. There are many societies that do not want anyone not "of the blood" to tell their tales. The fact that they were collected and put into books during a time in which other cultures were not fully respected may (or may not) be relevant. Even recently, in the early days of the Internet, several tribes put up Web sites with stories on them, which were pulled off after other people misused those stories. So be respectful enough to find out the situation.

Another major issue is which *version* to tell. Storytelling is a living art in that it is still going, but it is also a live art, meaning that it is at its best being performed in person. Recording "for posterity" is very valuable and provides interesting data for the researcher but live performances are much better. Similarly, getting wedded to a particular version of a story happens in collecting stories. First, we are dependent on the collector. The Grimm brothers did a wonderful thing by collecting ancient stories that might otherwise have been lost as fewer people remained in the pre-literate peasantry that kept storytelling alive. The cost was that these stories were filtered by humans who were very much part of the Victorian society around them. This meant that they disapproved of sexual material and were far from feminist in their outlook. So our view of the material collected comes through that filter. Only a few of those stories stayed alive in other versions, and most of those were lost as soon as the person who knew them happened upon the version known and "authorized" by others. In other words, if you will excuse my making up a word, they were to some extent "literacized" or turned into formal literature. We don't know much of what was lost, only that versions were lost.

In contrast, anthropological versions of stories as told by the people themselves are fascinating but not always easy to tell. One of my favorite stories about the issue is sheer gossip. Apparently a well-known anthropologist collecting in Alaska was told a story that included names of characters that were actually very insulting aspersions cast on the collector's mother. A picture book of that version is well known and still provides snickers to those in the know, while others revere it as true folklore.

Many cultures tell stories about well-known characters as they would anecdotes about friends and neighbors. You are expected to know the who, the where, and the what of the personalities, values, and expectations of the characters. These stories do not use the story form we are used to from European tales with a beginning, middle, and end. Also, cultural language norms vary. Some storytellers tell things straightforwardly, as if to establish that they were not lies but just normal speech. In other cultures the teller might be expected to use "fancy" language with extravagant words in elaborate sentences, because stories are a form of magic that requires the use of imagination. So, in our terms, the concern is that material gathered in the the mid-nineteenth century and trapped in the language of that era, which liked long and fancy versions, may not seem appealing today.

Also, to go back to the earlier anthropological note, many older print versions of tribal material were translated by those who had adopted the standard culture of their day. So someone might be born Algonquin but write like the Victorian gentleman he became. Our era will undoubtedly go out of fashion as well, along with our versions of stories, but for the moment we are concerned with deciding when to adopt something as is, when to adapt it, and when to abandon a version of a story. Appendix A at the back of this book generally has "tellable" versions, but it is a good idea to look for other versions and compare them if you find a story you like.

Let's look at two versions of the same tale, quite similar, but different in language and tone.

Anansi and the Dispersal of Wisdom

Another story tells of how Anansi once tried to hoard all of the world's wisdom in a pot [a calabash in some versions]. Anansi was already very clever, but he decided to gather together all the wisdom he could find and keep it in a safe place.

With all the wisdom sealed in a pot, he was still concerned that it was not safe enough, so he secretly took the pot to a tall thorny tree in the forest [in some versions the silk cotton tree]. His young son, Ntikuma, saw him go and followed him at some distance to see what he was doing.

The pot was too big for Anansi to hold while he climbed the tree, so he tied it in front of him. Like this, the pot was in the way and Anansi kept slipping, getting more and more frustrated and angry with each attempt.

Ntikuma laughed when he saw what Anansi was doing. "Why don't you tie the pot behind you, then you will be able to grip the tree?" he suggested.

Anansi was so annoyed by his failed attempts and the realization that his child was right that he let the pot slip. It smashed and all the wisdom fell out. Just at this moment, a storm arrived and the rain washed the wisdom into the stream. It was taken out to sea and spread all around the world so that there is now a little of it in everyone.

Though Anansi chased his son home through the rain, he was reconciled to the loss, for, he says: "What is the use of all that wisdom if a young child still needs to put you right?"[5]

Here is another version of the same story with different language and a different closing. Just think about what suits you personally, and where you might find one or the other more useful.

Why Wisdom Is Everywhere

A long time ago, Anansi the spider had all the wisdom in the world stored in a huge pot. Nyame, the sky god, had given it to him. Anansi had been instructed to share it with everyone.

Every day, Anansi looked in the pot and learned different things. The pot was full of wonderful ideas and skills.

Anansi greedily thought, "I will not share the treasure of knowledge with everyone. I will keep all the wisdom for myself."

So Anansi decided to hide the wisdom on top of a tall tree. He took some vines and made some strong string and tied it firmly around the pot, leaving one end free. He then tied the loose end around his waist so that the pot hung in front of him.

He then started to climb the tree. He struggled as he climbed because the pot of wisdom kept getting in his way, bumping against his tummy.

Anansi's son watched in fascination as his father struggled up the tree. Finally, Anansi's son told him, "If you tie the pot to your back, it will be easier to cling to the tree and climb."

Anansi tied the pot to his back instead and continued to climb the tree, with much more ease than before.

When Anansi got to the top of the tree, he became angry. "A young one with some common sense knows more than I, and I have the pot of wisdom!"

In anger, Anansi threw down the pot of wisdom. The pot broke, and pieces of wisdom flew in every direction. People found the bits scattered everywhere, and if they wanted, they could take some home to their families and friends.

That is why, to this day, no one person has *all* the world's wisdom. People everywhere share small pieces of it whenever they exchange ideas.[6]

Let's continue with another example that demonstrates a couple of things about differing versions. One of my favorite stories as a child was "Tikki Tikki Tembo." In the story, the boy with a short name is rescued from the well, but his brother, named "*Tikki-tikki-tembo No sa rembo Hari bari brooshki Peri pen do Hiki pon pom Nichi no miano Dom boriko*" drowned because when his brother shouted for help, his name took too long to say. It was supposed to be a silly story. In 1968, a picture book came out about *Tikki Tikki Tembo No Sa Rembo Hari Bari Ruchi Pip Peri Pembo*, in which he did not die, just took a long, long time to recover. Now this version is so well known in the United States that it is hard to tell the older version. The original story is part of the Japanese tradition of starting a storytelling session with a very silly story to get the group together with a laugh; the newer version reflects the attitude in America at the time in which children were not supposed to die. That change of attitudes from one culture or era to another is an important issue. Another issue that is related to this story is that people with sensitivity to racism have been known to react with anger to the tale. My friend and storytelling student founded a site dealing with children's literature where there is a discussion of this very situation.[7] It is important to understand that one must pay attention to such things. Usually, if you introduce the story by talking about the Japanese tradition, such anger is prevented but first, be warned that one can unintentionally offend people, and second, recognize the importance of knowing the culture of the story as well as the story itself. The anthropologist Eliot Singer has written an angry article on the Web about the disrespect of many children's books for the cultures they take material from.[8] You must decide for yourself but it needs thought.

Another story that I loved to hear and to tell is an old English folktale called "The Hobyahs," a silly, scary story in which the Hobyahs "eat up the old man, eat up the old woman, and carry off the little girl."[9] A recent picture book version softens the story and, in my eyes, ruins it. Why? Children ordinarily don't seem bothered by violence in stories. The fact that they see and hear a great deal of violence on the news may mean that facing a little in a safe environment can be a relief. Adults, however, want to protect them and you must know your listeners before you decide whether to tell the original version. If there is a chance that children with a background of abuse are present, don't tell such stories. As a storyteller you must decide what works for both you as teller and your audience—both the children and the group with its adult affiliations.

You will find many stories that come in equally dramatically different versions of the plot. There are even more that come in both long versions and short ones, and some in fancy language or plain words. It is worth researching before you decide to invest the time in learning a story.

Finally comes the issue of whether or not to memorize. This is my take on it: Kipling, Sandburg, and Andersen all wrote with carefully chosen words. If the story is an original story, you memorize it. If you choose to tell their stories, learn them word for word. Period. Several students over the years have done so and performed wonderfully and gone on to share those stories with many audiences. Such performances draw my deep admiration. I also have memorized several stories verbatim over the years and am proud of them.

In the old days of library storytelling, you memorized any story you told. Like being an actor, it went with the job. That went for any story you told from a book—and that was the only kind allowed. Augusta Baker, Naomi Noyes, Ellin Greene, and Caroline Field were marvelous storytellers and memorized every word. A few others recited like automatons until they became comfortable—if they ever did. Still, the point was that they saw themselves as "missionaries of the printed word" as it were, and a child deserved to find the story in the book the same as the one they had heard. This will ring true to anyone who has had a child demand the same story again and again and become very upset if a line is changed.

According to psychologists, young children really do find suspense in stories they have heard many times. They think and hope that this time the Three Billy Goats Gruff will escape, but they are not sure and feel real anxiety until they hear the resolution. That is part of the fun of telling to young children. It does require being able to tell a story in the same way, again and again. Adults today, on the other hand, tend to be annoyed by repetition, so the style of telling to them is as different as the content of their stories.

Today, many people find it hard to memorize. One has a little lee-way with a folk tale since you, too, are a member of the "folk." So if it was collected by the Brothers Grimm, by Asbjørnsen and Moe, or an anthropologist, be respectful but don't kill yourself if you forget an exact phrase. (If you are confused about who is an author and who is a collector, look in the library: if it is shelved as a 398, it is considered folklore.) If you don't have access to a good library, know that there are many Web sites that have folklore. You will find them at the end of the bibliography.

After all this warning, let me just give one last piece of advice: don't be careless, certainly don't be disrespectful of either the culture or the collector, learn the story and its language and a little about its background, but at the same time don't be obsessive-compulsive about word-for-word memorization or anthropological purity. The world has great need for the warmth and enjoyment of storytelling; therefore, there is a greater need for occasionally imperfect story sharers than for a few storytelling idiots savants.

Appendix A, found at the end of this book, is a list of stories from which to choose. They have been proven with audiences, but there is nothing wrong with starting with family or personal favorites. The list does not include recordings, but there are many fine ones available commercially or on the Internet.

EXERCISE

Look at the storiography and choose a few stories or collections to browse through, looking for a tale you might like to tell.

NOTES

1. Barry McWilliams. This was on his old Web site, www.eldrbarry.net (February 1998). His current site is www.eldrbarry.net/roos/eest.htm.

2. Angela Lansbury, in an interview with Robert Osborne from Turner Classic Movies, 2006.

3. Jon Scieszka, *The True Story of the Three Little Pigs* (New York: Viking, 1989).

4. *Seanachie* is pronounced "shawnakhee," I have been told by Irish tellers.

5. Taken from Martha Warren Beckwith, *Jamaica Anansi Stories* (New York: Memoirs of the American Folk-lore Society, Stechert & Co., 1924). Available at en.wikipedia.org/wiki/Anansi (July 16, 2010).

6. www.motherlandnigeria.com/stories/why_wisdom_is_everywhere.html (July 16, 2010).

7. www.fairrosa.info/disc/tikki.html (February 4, 2010).

8. www.msu.edu/user/singere/fakelore.html (June 20, 2010).

9. Joseph Jacobs, *More English Fairy Tales* (Mattituck, NY: Amereon, 1894), 270.

CHAPTER 7

Building a Program

There is no merit in ninety-nine stories out of one hundred except the merit put into them by the teller's art.

— Mark Twain

Telling individual stories is fine, but if you are going to do it for groups, they will usually ask for a program. There are many ways of approaching a program. If it is for younger children, you will probably find that some kind of activity is a good thing to integrate with the stories. This is because young children have a great deal of energy and are not used to sitting still for long periods. There are stories that contain interaction within them, like phrases that are repeated by the audience or questions that are answered by them, but I am talking about physical activities that involve standing up.

Be careful what you choose, because doing something too active can make it hard to switch gears back to quietly sitting and listening. It pays to pay attention to transitions and the impact of various activities.

Here is a simple standing-up stretch, for example:

Reach up high, high, high
to the sky, sky, sky.
Then reach wide, wide, wide
to each side, side, side.
Then bow low, low, low
to the floo[r], floo[r], floo[r].
Now we sit, sit, sit,
And use our wit, wit, wit.

Here is a song with motions:

I'm a little teapot, short and stout.
Here is my handle,
   [*hold one arm akimbo with hand touching the side below the waist*]
And here is my spout.
   [*hold one arm up at an angle to represent the spout*]
When I get all steamed up, here me *shout!*
Just tip me over
   [*bend to the side*]
and pour me out.
   [*tilt to the side,* then stand up straight afterward]

Such simple games do not set up interaction between children, which is good because they can find that very distracting. The point is to prevent discomfort from sitting still too long. There are many such games explained in books and on the web. *Juba This and Juba That* is one of my favorite collections, but there are many others as well.[1]

Most preschool groups do better with picture books on which to focus, so a mix of reading, storytelling, and games works well. There are many storytellers who refuse to do actual formal telling to anyone younger than the age of about eight, simply because many young children find it hard to react to something so different from the world they already know. My feeling is that it is very difficult to work with children so young with storytelling, but at the same time, this is where you can reach into the future by developing an audience who will take to storytelling as normal.

I do not like to use such games with older children, even those in primary grades, because they are distracting and it is so important for children to learn that plain-voice stories can be fascinating and pleasurable. The reality is that they enjoy picture books and games, which makes it very appealing to use them, and they are so much less effort for the presenter. Please do not get seduced by their ease, however, because *story listening* is something that is really important to encourage. Constant distraction is the normal pattern of attention today, so the art of developing concentration is a real gift to give children. Reality is reality, however, and it is sometimes necessary to use participation stories. Even the purest of storytellers is wise, particularly when starting off, to have several such stories on hand to use since it takes time to develop a full repertoire of stories for all occasions. There are audiences that are just not ready for steady listening.

Caroline Feller Bauer did several books of such programs with activities and stories interlaced.[2] We used to argue against using such activities, but I have become convinced that there are times when they are good to use. Caroline was much loved as a storyteller and used to travel to international sites as well as local ones with a whole trunk full of goodies: musical instruments, toys, dolls, costumes, and so on. She felt that the world was so full of distractions that stories needed to have them as well. She had an "if you can't lick 'em, join 'em" attitude and was great fun to be with. She saw storytelling as primarily entertaining, with learning hidden inside, like putting vitamins inside fancy desserts. She was grateful for the training she had gotten at the New York Public Library, even though she took a different path.

I know someone else who uses a bag with little things in it. Someone from the audience is allowed to reach in and "choose" the story it represents. I know someone else who uses different pebbles and says that each represents a story. The choice is actually made by the teller, which feels a little dishonest to me, but it pleases children with the sense of power to choose.

Really great storytellers of the likes of Augusta Baker could catch and keep any group's attention with their voices and tales. That is the best. At the same time, be realistic and recognize that you can only get to be best with practice. When you know the group, it is much easier to do straight telling, because they know what to expect, but when you are presenting to a new group, it is wise to be prepared with a few alternatives in case they turn out to be new to storytelling and need a break from listening. Do not become dependent on props and games; recognize them as a crutch for the teller and a distraction for the audience, but do have them available for emergencies—and for fun.

At the same time, people who like stories tend to like symbolic traditions as well. One thing the New York Public Library did, and I have continued in my classes, is lighting a candle at the beginning of the program. Storytelling began at the New York Public Library as a result of Anne Carroll Moore's attendance at a storytelling performance at a "white gloves" occasion at a fancy hotel where young ladies and gentlemen were being entertained. It was before World War I, and she was developing the idea of library service for children. This struck her as a brilliant way to accomplish several things. First, children from peasant backgrounds, whether European, Caribbean, or Asian, needed to learn how to function in American society. They were asked to get tickets days before the story "concert" and stood in line before being invited into the story hour theater. This was to prepare them for going to the theater for concerts, plays, or films.

That is no longer needed in the way it was then, since most people have taken their children at least to the movies today. But it does still bring the sense of occasion to a library story hour. The second idea was in a way the reverse of the first one. Instead of integrating children into New York life, it was to bring the culture of their own backgrounds into the library. Hearing stories from one's native culture in English in the library made it seem appropriate to admire that culture and per- haps made it easier to learn English. At the same time, it also allowed children from one group to get to know the culture and values of other groups. Something else that developed was "trading programs": be- cause it took considerable effort to learn several stories for a program, the storytellers would trade programs, going to different libraries to perform for a different audience. This made it more formal and also gave children the chance to hear different storytellers with different backgrounds and telling styles. Perhaps you could adapt such a trading arrangement with other tellers in related settings—Scouting troops, Sunday Schools, and so forth.

This reminds me of a story another professor told me. She and her sister arrived in New York from Hungary one summer just before World War II. Her parents did not know any English and worried about how the girls would do in school, so they told them to pay attention to the other children playing in the streets so that they could pick up some English. They learned a little over the summer, so they headed for school with some comfort.

Once they got to school, they saw many of the children they knew from the streets, and that made them feel even better. Then the teacher began to speak. They did not understand a word and wondered what their "friends" had done to them. Then they looked over at those friends and saw them looking back with equally stunned expressions. Their new friends were from Italy and had been picking up Hungarian, think-ing it was English, just as the sisters had been learning Italian, thinking that it was English.

That experience is still being repeated in many parts of the country, and it underlines the point about introducing other cultures. Values, types of humor, and ways of interacting can be picked up from stories, and the issue of respecting other traditions is just as important as it was during the earlier waves of immigration.

To get back to the New York Public Library pattern of story pro-grams: a candle was lit at the beginning of each storytelling perfor-mance. They represented the old fire, whether a campfire or a fireplace fire, by which storytelling used to take place. It was a token that captured the spirit of the magic of a story occasion. It was also a good division between "story time" and "normal time." Once the candle was lit, only the storyteller spoke. When the stories ended and the candle extinguished, it made a good transition back into normal time. It gave the storyteller a moment to recollect him- or herself and the listeners a chance to absorb the story and also to change gears.

Many storytellers took that moment to ask the audience to close their eyes, make a wish, and then blow out the candle. The storyteller blows out the candle for safety, but, symbolically, everyone does. Depending on the circumstances and one's personal tastes, it is okay to prompt the wishes with a comment like, "if you are willing to wish for world peace rather than for something for yourself, that would be wonderful." It depends on you and your sense of the occasion.

Someone found a storyteller's stool from West Africa for me, and students in class really enjoy having it. Such a thing could be seen as going against the "let the stories speak for themselves" policy, but it feels good to have this connection from one year to another. I have never used it when invited to tell stories, but it feels good in the class, when everyone is full of nerves and excitement and is being inducted into the world of people known as "storytellers."

So, if you want to have a tradition, either personal or within an insti-tution, feel free to adopt these, if something else does not develop. If it does, welcome it, for it will give you much pleasure.

To get back to the idea of program planning, one "tradition" to pass on is the idea of having a few stories tucked away that you know are always a hit. If the audience does not respond to those, then you know that it is the audience that is the "dud" and feel better. On the rare occasion when that happens, you can switch to something like a participation story in which the audience plays a part or something funny that will get them to participate with laughter. Having an emergency back-up plan can really ease anxiety with an unknown audience.

Bumps happen. You never know when a story you have chosen will turn out to be inappropriate. It does happen occasionally. For example, I have often told "Tom Tit Tot," a British variant of "Rumpelstiltskin," and it is usually very well-received. It begins by introducing the girl who is "gatless," which basically means witless. At one performance, I had begun the story when a girl in the audience got up and started walking around. It was very clear that she was both mentally handicapped and emotionally disturbed. It was too late to stop the story, and I had to revise it so that the class would not picture her as that character. Luckily, I saw that girl early enough and shortened the funny parts emphasizing the character's lack of knowledge and sophistication to get to the part where she wins over Tom Tit Tot and the mean king. But you cannot know if someone's parent just died, if a child is deathly afraid of snakes, and so on. Just know that occasionally you will get signals that something is not working well, and if that happens, shorten the story drastically ("so, after many other adventures, it was all straightened out, and he married the princess, and they all lived happily ever after") and then tell a different one. The idea is to plan wonderful programs but always have a "bolt-hole" alternate to pull out of your hat.

Another major issue is selecting stories that are appropriate for a particular age group. Younger children like repetition and stories that deal with issues that are developmentally appropriate. In other words, don't tell a story about a couple deciding to separate or a story about aging and death to young children. I remember when Dr. Seuss's *Butter Battle Book* first came out.[3] Having been invited to a party to meet Dr. Seuss and getting a signed copy of the book seemed a real opportunity to share the book with the school at which I was school librarian. So I read it to all the classes, kindergarten through seventh grade. It was a fascinating experience, one that brought home developmental issues. The younger boys were all about choosing one side or the other and fighting for bread that was "butter side up" or "butter side down," although the point of the book was a pacifist message about the silliness of escalating a disagreement over such an issue. It was not until third grade that some got the point, and by fourth grade almost all had gotten the point. Clearly a developmental point was being reached then. This is not a book about developmental psychology, but you do need to think about such things when developing programs. If it feels unintuitive to you, reading a textbook chapter on the theories of Piaget, Kohlberg, and others can be helpful.

It is also important to consider language and usage. I can remember getting angry at my mother and stomping down the hill on the way to nursery school when I was four, because she said something had happened "last Thursday." I knew what "last" meant, and I also knew that tomorrow would be Thursday again, so how could a week ago have been the "last" Thursday? Maybe because she had been in the hospital for a few weeks explained my overreaction, but it provides a good example of the difference of a child's point of view.

For another example of a child's perspective, there is the anecdote from a friend who told me about being given a puppy for Christmas when she was quite young.[4] She got very worried when the puppy got sick, but when she was told that he was going to be taken to the "dog doctor," she got upset and fussed. As they were getting ready to go, she said, "but Daddy, how will the dog doctor be able to tell us what's wrong?" At that moment, he understood that she thought the doctor was a dog, not that he was a human doctor for dogs. He was kind enough to explain, though he started to laugh. The point is that children have a very different perspective, and you cannot always know how they will respond. So be open, after the story, to answer questions.

Traditional nursery stories have worked many of these issues out, which is a good reason for using them, even if they are "old hat." "If it ain't broke, don't fix it" [or replace it], particularly for young children who are not yet concerned with fashion. There are good recent stories, also, like the song-story "Abiyoyo," but there are so many wonderful modern picture books to provide contemporary entertainment that it seems better to start with proven traditional story material for telling.

There are other occasions that are very formal, where you are expected to tell specific stories and are not welcome to deviate. I told a few stories at "The Egg," a theater at the state capital in Albany, New

York, along with other tellers, and in that kind of a situation you tell the story you were invited to tell within the time that was allotted for it. Again, it can happen that you get a little nervous and speed up, which means that you finish more quickly than usual. If an exact amount of time was allotted, say a class period, you need to fill it. Sometimes you can invite questions, sometimes you can fill time talking about the stories or storytelling. At other times, the story is such that its impact would be destroyed by idle chitchat. In such a situation, it is better to break and walk off the stage. There is nothing to prevent you from getting back onstage after a minute or two as applause dies down, at which time you can talk about the story.

It is generally more of a problem to exceed the allotted time, particularly if several people are performing or if you are in a school with regular class periods. Few things are worse than having students get up and leave before you have finished a story and, believe me, they will. So it is a good idea to think beforehand about what bits of the story could be dropped if necessary or abbreviated. Not ideal, but adequate. For example, listing all the characters who came to the wedding of the protagonists in a love story could be bypassed. No matter how carefully you have timed stories when learning them, it will happen on occasion that they will need to be shortened or lengthened. The simplest thing, of course, is just to slow down or speed up your telling. If you have timed a story and know that you have reached the halfway point and are less or more than halfway through the time allotted to the story, that is your cue to speed up or slow down. At this point, it can still be done without making the audience feel that you are racing through the story or having trouble remembering it.

As you get more experienced and skilled, you will find yourself asked to take on larger audiences, for example, an auditorium full of children rather than an individual classroom. Usually it means a more diverse group, as well, and you must choose stories that will work for all. Generally, you need to start with something that appeals to a wide group, and then you can slip in one for the younger children, maybe with repetition, and then switch to a more sophisticated one that includes elements appealing to younger children but with ideas that stimulate older children's thinking.

Designing a successful program is a different issue than choosing individual stories that suit your style, but it is also a very important aspect of storytelling. We have talked of trying to choose stories that suit you, but it is also important to consider the pace of a complete program. Pacing involves the style in which a story is told. Some have a slow, even pace, some build to a climax that leads the teller to speed up and maybe use a louder voice. There are a number of Halloween stories that build to a scream, others that are choppy as they build to a smooth ending. Depending on the occasion and the length of the program, you may feel it is wise to change pace, or it may be that a special occasion (for example, a wedding) calls for a single tone and style.

It is not enough to choose stories around a theme. Part of the issue is choosing the order in which to tell stories. One useful pattern begins with a story that is reassuring to the audience by making them feel that listening to you is safe and worth the effort. Then you want to make them feel that they have learned something and are smarter than they were before listening. Finally, they are ready for a story that will move them. Elizabeth Ellis calls this the "*Ha ha / Aha / Aaah*" pattern. As with all suggestions, this is for getting started. You may well develop your own patterns over time as you become more skilled.

There is no one program or plan that is right. It depends on who you are, who the audience is, what occasion is being celebrated (if any), and the setting (inside, outside, with or without mike, with or without outside distractions, such as in a shopping center).

So, how do you design a program? Themes can cover almost any topic. It can be something like stories from a particular culture or area, stories that deal with an issue like romance or loss, or stories that involve some activity like cooking or science. Just "my favorite stories" works. The point is that having some kind of theme makes for a better program. Just as a meal can be based on a particular country's cuisine, traditional dishes for a holiday, or someone's favorites and be a wonderful feast, all kinds of combinations can make for great entertainment. It depends only on the imagination of the teller in tying it all together.

One can use some stories in many situations, for they can connect in different ways. For example, a favorite story of mine is one of an emperor who holds a contest for children that involves planting and tending a seed. He promises to judge the results. Many children join the contest, and their parents help by providing elegant flowerpots and sometimes by helping with watering and tending. Some parents even plant new seeds when they don't see any seedlings in the pot after a few weeks so that their children won't be discouraged or embarrassed. At last comes the day for judging, and all the children show up with their pretty plants, except for one boy who had a plain pot. The emperor looks at all the plants and the proud parents, and then goes to the boy with the empty pot. The boy says, simply, "I watered it and tended it, but nothing came up." The emperor then says, "This is the boy I want as a member of my court; he was the only one who was honest. The seeds were cooked before they were handed out, so they could not grow." So the honest boy was rewarded. This is the version set in China and told by Demi in her picture book, *The Empty Pot*, which tells it beautifully.[5] There are other versions of this story in which the parents are not as involved and it is the children themselves who decide to cheat.

Now if you were using this in a Sunday School or church setting, it would make good sense to tell the parable of sowing seed, where some falls on rock, some on arid land, and some falls on good soil and takes root.

If, on the other hand, you were learning about China in school, you might want to pair this story with another story from a different part of China. Or, if it were spring, you might connect it with another story about growing things and use that as the theme. Do you understand the principle? One can connect by topic, by theme, by place of origin, or anything else you can come up with. It just makes the transition from one story to the next easier.

As I mentioned earlier, you can find very different versions of the same tale. *Stone Soup* is a good example of this. The basic story involves a group of soldiers who are hungry. They come to a town but are unsuccessful at getting something to eat from the peasants. One of the soldiers then says that he has a soup stone and offers to make soup for the whole village. People are skeptical, but they can't help being curious. Gradually, they "remember" that they have an onion, a few turnips, a couple of carrots, and so on. A big kettle is produced and the soup starts cooking. Needless to say, it ends up being a party with a delicious soup. Now, the version I first heard was from a picture book by Marcia Brown, another New York Public Library storyteller, who set it in a French village after the Napoleonic wars, but she was obviously reacting to the time in which she produced the book, which was shortly after World War II.[6] Another picture book version, *Nail Soup*, sets it in Scandinavia, with an old lady being fooled by a tramp.[7] A more recent *Stone Soup* sets the same story in Asia, with monks teaching villagers.[8] All are good, but they are quite different.

Now, I have not told this story often, and although I have not researched it, I assume that it is a story that has versions from various parts of Europe. If you are planning to use this story as a lesson about Asian cultures, you would be very wrong, for it was just adapted for that book, and the notes say so. If, on the other hand, if you want to use it as part of a program about values, to be followed with a discussion of fooling people, it would be great, even in a Zen community, for the theme suits that discussion. Different settings have different requirements, relating to a story's background, its theme, or even to something else entirely.

This is all relevant to designing programs. There is nothing wrong with declaring your theme to be "my favorite stories"; it does not have to have a lesson attached, but most audiences will expect a theme of some kind.

Let's consider theme. What are you particularly interested in? It could be dogs. There are stories about dog fights. There is the story about why the dog has a cold wet nose (from plugging a hole on Noah's ark—a *pourquoi* story from Ireland). There are stories about loyal dogs from all over the world, such as the story of Jojofu from Japan and the tragic mediaeval ballad of "Beth Gelert" (in which a dog is killed by his master because he thinks it attacked his son, but the dog actually fought off a wolf that attacked the son).[9] Then there are amusing stories, like "Why Dog Hates the Cat," a funny tale about the rivalry between the two and what started it.[10] These all have very different themes, but all are about dogs. You could use dogs as the theme and select some of these or use one of them in a program about loyalty or stories from a particular place.

Going in a different direction, you could partner one of my favorite Chinese stories, "Man in the Moon," with any number of other stories. "Man in the Moon" is about generosity and selfishness in a very clear lesson, but it is also very charming. Two friends, one rich, one poor, walk in the woods together and find a wounded bird. The poor one takes it home to help it while its wing heals, and the rich one says that his friend is being foolish. Then the bird rewards the poor friend, and the rich friend decides to try the same thing. He ends up on the moon, looking for gold. You could pair it with stories about kindness, generosity, or stinginess. (I often pair it with a very silly story from Japan about a stingy landlord.) Or you could pair it with another story from China or another story about the moon. Or with the story about the starfish in chapter 13. In one story, the protagonist is rewarded with money, in the other with only the knowledge that he helped, but they are similar in intent. The possibilities are broad; it just takes a storyteller's mind and imagination to see the connections.

In class, I have students select stories with a theme. In addition to lists of stories from a particular country or culture, I have had students produce "storiographies" about cooking, law, honesty, and death, as well as stories about the "evil eye," and dragon stories from different parts of the world, illustrating the difference in attitudes toward dragons between the East and the West. Some design fancy programs and give them to the audience, others just present the spoken program. It is a matter of choice, but again it is good practice to be prepared for those occasions when a particular set of stories or activities has been chosen by the organization hiring you. Having a selection of programs to choose from makes you look professional. Do be warned that you can prepare for one audience, only to find quite a different audience. That is why we discussed having emergency back-up programs. The need for back-up stories doesn't happen often, but it is best to be prepared.

One thing that librarian storytellers do that most others don't is show a copy of the book from which a story was taken. This is done to allow children to read a story they had just heard and find other similar ones. Of course, books are no longer the only source of stories, and you will have to decide how to deal with that, but the principle that children should be informed about the books and cultures that are sources of stories is still important. It is too easy in the current environment to accept it all as "free for the taking" instead of as a gift from the past.

Whether you are telling as a volunteer or as a professional, remember that stories connect us with the earth as a whole and that this is not the first time that humans have experienced great change. It is cyclical.

I have always loved the Chinese curse: "May you live in interesting times." If we can keep in mind that saying about the storyteller's voice expressing the heartbeat of the Earth Mother, Gaia, and maintain our storytelling at a dignified level, allowing it to be fast and hard when appropriate but generally leaving the manic pace and high blood pressure sensationalism to the media, we should be able to build an interesting era that is fun to live in, rather than a curse.

Certainly we are in very interesting times right now, and it is important that we remember our humanity. Great creativity is always freed in such eras, and as long as we maintain harmony and build new forms of creativity with trust and balance in order to keep it flowing like a river instead of always trying to create dams of control, we may start a whole new era of good times.

It is fascinating to see how home videos are being included in television news, be it disaster or weather. News is changing, and ordinary individuals are reporting what is happening on their cell phones. Producers and news commentators can edit them, but anyone interested can find out more from the Internet. Perhaps this will have the effect of making things come back down to human levels. Maybe texting will make written communication seem more personal to future generations so that texted versions of storytelling will feel more natural. For now, it is important to honor our traditions and tell stories in ways that support life.

Know that nothing will replace the pleasure of hearing stories together with others. Even though other story forms may compete for our attention, we are built to enjoy hearing stories as a group.

EXERCISES

Think about one or two themed programs for young children, maybe using tales and activities you remember from your own early childhood—like "I'm a little teapot" or "going on a bear hunt."

Think about a program for teens. What would you like to address? Their heritage? Some issue they are dealing with? Something else?

Think about a program for adults. If you were using the same theme, how would it differ from the program for teens?

NOTES

1. Virginia Tashjian, *Juba This and Juba That: Stories to Tell, Songs to Sing, Rhymes to Chant, Riddles to Guess and More* (Boston: Little, Brown, 1995).

2. Caroline Feller Bauer, *New Handbook for Storytellers with Stories, Poems, Magic and More* (Chicago: American Language Association, 1993).

3. Theodore Seuss Geisel, *Butter Battle Book* (New York: Random House, 1984).

4. Susan O'Dell told me this in 2010.

5. Demi, *Empty Pot* (New York: Henry Holt, 1990). Again, it is better to learn from plain versions, but sometimes it is good to know about easily found versions in picture books.

6. Marcia Brown, *Stone Soup* (New York: Atheneum, 1947).

7. Harve Zemach, *Nail Soup: A Swedish Tale* (Chicago: Follett, 1964). Still other versions include Eric Maddern, *Nail Soup* (London: Frances Lincoln, 2009); Heather Forest and Susan Gaber, *Stone Soup* (Little Rock, AR: August House, 1998); and Tony Ross, *Stone Soup* (New York: Puffin, 1992), who has a hen fending off the wolf with her stone soup.

8. Jon J. Muth, *Stone Soup* (New York: Scholastic, 2003).

9. *Beth Gelert; or, the Grave of the Greyhound*, by William Robert Spencer (1769–1834).

10. In Zora Neal Hurston, *Of Mules and Men* (New York: Harper Perennial, 1990), 159; also as "Why Dogs Hate Cats," in Julius Lester's *The Knee-High Man and Other Tales* (New York: Dial, 1972).

CHAPTER 8

Performance Issues

I never knew how much thought went into telling a story. It's hard, but it was fun. I was so nervous when I first got up to tell my story, but by the end of the week I actually enjoyed telling it. If I can do that I think I can do anything.

—an eighth-grade student[1]

One issue that needs to be addressed head-on is the anxiety that many people feel as they talk to groups. It is said that this is the greatest fear most people have, but it needn't be traumatic if you can translate it into excitement. Anticipation can trip you up, but if you can recognize that this is your body's way of getting ready for a time that you will be using adrenaline and see it as part of the preparation, you should be fine.[2]

On the other hand, there are many who enjoy talking to groups, and others who have a sense of fun that makes such fears seem ludicrous. Last summer a student spoke about how she had embarrassed her family at Disney World by accepting an invitation from Mickey Mouse to dance with him in a parade. Funny, isn't it, how different people with the same genes can be? A fair number of storytellers also perform as clowns or magicians and mix their performances. A wonderful ventriloquist, Jay Johnson, performed on Broadway not too long ago, and I was amazed to see how he included storytelling in his performance and to what great effect.[3]

There are advantages to performance anxiety. Most performers feel some anxiety before each gig and find that the adrenaline makes them perform better—just as stockbrokers seem to do better if their adrenaline is running. I am not sure what the comparison is, but risk taking can be found in many forms.

Sometimes just knowing that such anxiety is normal is enough to allow you to ignore or forget about it. There are people who are attracted to storytelling in order to get over such anxiety. They are more than welcome. You are presenting the story for attention to that story, not for attention to yourself, so it can be a good way to help yourself while giving to others. In chapter 2, we discussed Toastmasters groups, but they can help with the anxiety aspect of storytelling because they give practice talking to groups so that it can feel normal rather than stressful.

The old advice about imagining the audience naked still works for some. I prefer finding a face in the audience that looks friendly and responsive and aiming most of my attention there. It is interesting how other people in the audience find that pleasant. You do not have to look everyone in the eye, but they feel "seen" if you look at at least one person or, better yet, one person in each area of the audience. If you seem too anxious, the audience will pick up on it and become anxious themselves, and no one will enjoy the experience. If you find yourself getting anxious, don't freak out, but say "whoops" internally and smile as you laugh at yourself for getting anxious. It really is not that big a deal.

One of my storytelling students introduced me to Dorothy Sarnoff's book, *Never Be Nervous Again.*[4] Sarnoff taught public speaking to many famous people who had to address groups. The trick is a simple way to block the formation of noradrenaline or epinephrine. It sounds a little strange at first but this is what she says to do with your "innards" to deal with the stress:

> To understand how these muscles [the rectus abdominis] work, try this. Sit down in a straight-backed chair. Carry your rib cage high, but not so high you're in a ramrod-straight military position. Incline slightly forward. Now put your hands together out in front of you, your elbows akimbo, your fingers pointing upward, and push so that you feel an isometric opposing force in the heels of your palms and under your arms.
>
> Say *ssssssss*, like a hiss. As you're exhaling the *s*, contract those muscles in the vital triangle as though you were rowing a boat against a current, pulling the oars back and up. Now the vital triangle should feel like you're tightening a corset. Relax the muscles at the end of your exhalation, then inhale gently.

Contracting those muscles prevents the production of noradrenaline or epinephrine, the fear-producing chemicals in your system. While you're waiting to go on, sit with your vital triangle contracting, you're lips slightly parted, releasing your breath over your teeth in a silent *sssss*. You can do it anywhere, without anyone noticing. And nothing, absolutely nothing will be able to make you nervous.[5]

If and when you become a professional storyteller, and a fair number of you may do so, then you can worry about your performance, but until then don't worry about people looking a gift horse in the mouth. People love to hear stories; even those told less than perfectly. One of the issues about storytelling is that it is a living performance and a folk art, like cooking. There are professional chefs on television, but most of us eat such food only on rare, special occasions. Always remember that you are offering a gift; it is no shame to you if someone does not like chocolate or if you happen to cook beef Stroganoff for a group that no one told you were vegetarians. Just do your best. Most audiences will be welcoming and you will feel your effort was paid back with a great gain. Remember, "nothing ventured, nothing gained."

Most of you will be tellers for fun, but if you should decide to do it professionally, you must accept the responsibility of doing your best. If you are a volunteer, you may also find yourself telling to large groups, so the following exercise would be of value to you, too. A major concern is learning to project your voice so that all can hear and understand you. It is much harder with a large group than you might think. One exercise that you can do is to rehearse with a partner. Stand at opposite ends of a long hall. Take turns talking to each other and listen to how much effort it takes to be heard and understood. Not everyone has the same kind of voice, and some are heard more easily than others, and this will give you a sense of the issue as both speaker and hearer. The next thing to do is try it outside. Suddenly, you find your voice dissipating as it goes in many directions. Then find a room that has a loud air conditioner or something else that obscures sound and find out how that affects your voice and your hearing. If it is too hard to hear, people give up and you lose your audience.

Most stories have sections that call for a louder voice and sections that call for a quieter one. People are willing to listen harder for brief sections, but it must be hearable. Most people today are so used to overamplified sound that they find it difficult to listen too hard for very long.

Some people use a microphone, the way singers do, and there are occasions (like performing outside at a fair, for example) when they are necessary, but I prefer doing without one, just because I like to see storytelling as a way of proving people are not completely dependent on technology. One thing that you can do when preparing for a performance is to enlist an ally who will hold a hand to an ear if it is hard to hear from the back of a performance space, so you know to speak up. Some auditoriums are well designed so that a voice carries well, and some small spaces have acoustic tiles or other elements that swallow vocal sound.

There is another aspect of sound, that of enunciation. It used to be that declaiming/elocution, or what was later called "oral interpretation" was a required course for most students. In the days when only the upper classes got an education, learning how to speak well was part of that education. Such elocution is out of fashion now, and most of us know it only from the "One Grecian Urn" scene in *The Music Man*.[6]

I mentioned earlier an elementary school classmate who learned to recite pieces for an audience and who was punished with a strap if she did not do it well. It is so out of fashion now that it may seem funny, but public speaking may well be something that we have lost, much to our detriment. Certainly it would make storytelling easier if we all had elocution under our belts. Some drama departments still include voice classes, so you could explore those or find a textbook.

If you still are concerned about stage fright, relax. Sometimes you need to enchant yourself as well as the audience for a good performance. There is no harm in preparing yourself as a conduit for the stories, as long as part of you doesn't get carried away or drunk with self-importance. Think about the person who kept reminding Caesar and other conquering generals "you are mortal, remember you are mortal." As part of that mortality, recognize that after the performance, you should expect a let down. Whether or not you are running on adrenaline, you have exerted enormous energy, and it is normal to feel its loss. It is a good idea to have something planned afterward. For example, you might make plans to go out to dinner with someone who will listen to you talk yourself down from the occasion.

To prevent stage fright, here is a mantra or prayer that can help:

I am happy to be here.
I am happy that you are here to hear me.
I care about you, and want to share these stories,
as a gift, through me, from storytellers through the ages.[7]

Or, if you prefer, it makes perfect sense to change the last phrase to "from Gaia," "from the earth," "from the world," "from God," or whatever else feels appropriate to you and the occasion. Incidentally, this is a good example of the conflict between live storytelling with spoken words and the joint storehouse/prison of print: I hereby give you permission to take the idea, which I adapted from Sarnoff, and shape it to your own needs as a member of the fraternity of storytellers.

Remember, storytelling is fun for both teller and audience. Think of that poor centipede in the joke who was asked how he managed to walk with all those legs and, upon thinking about it, became so tangled up that he could not walk at all anymore. Forget the "issues," connect your whole body to the ground through your feet so that you don't feel as if you are floating away, set your mind on connecting with the audience, and enjoy it.

EXERCISE

Try writing your own mantra/prayer. Maybe you will come up with something that works better for you.

NOTES

1. Quoted in Martha Hamilton and Mitch Weiss, *Children Tell Stories: A Teaching Guide* (Katonah, NY: Richard C. Owen, 1990), 15.

2. I remember being the bridesmaid for someone who was a prize-winning athlete and being startled when this convent-raised girl started swearing a blue streak. She was fine at the ceremony, but maybe that was her way of releasing anxiety.

3. Part of the reason I remember him is that he sold a set of plastic eyes to be worn over the index finger and called them "Spaulding Eyes." I could not resist buying a set, although I have yet to use them.

4. Dorothy Sarnoff, *Never Be Nervous Again* (New York: Crown, 1987).

5. Sarnoff, *Never Be Nervous Again*, 68–69.

6. Meredith Willson, *The Music Man*. Story by Meredith Willson and Franklin Lacey. First performed on Broadway in 1957.

7. This is adapted from Sarnoff:

I'm glad I'm here.
I'm glad you're here.
I care about you.
I know that I know. (1987, 76)

CHAPTER 9

Interacting with the Audience

Three apples fell from heaven:
One for the storyteller,
One for the listener, and
One for the person who understands.

—Armenian saying[1]

Let's start with a story.

Touch of the Master/The Master's Touch

Once there was an auction; many goods had been sold and at a great price. Suddenly, the auctioneer picked an old violin and started auctioning it. Nobody showed interest in the violin. At last, somebody from the crowd placed a bid for $25 for the violin. Just as the auctioneer was about to seal the price, a dignified old man who had seen many years of life and was full of wisdom waved the auctioneer to wait. He took the old violin and wiped it clean. He started playing the violin. The melody that came out of the violin was enough to make angels dance. The place was very quiet as all enjoyed the melody. The old man gave back the violin to the auctioneer who started auctioning it. People started bidding $500, $1,000, $5,000, $15,000, $25,000, $50,000. "Oh!" exclaimed somebody in the crowd, "why has the violin's price gone so high?" The auctioneer responded, "because of the Master's touch."

The old man was the master who knew the purpose of the violin and knew that the dusty violin wasn't finished yet. He taught the people that the violin was still useful. There is nothing useless in this world; everything is useful. All that is needed is the touch of the master. When people are down and think life is over for them, the touch of the master can turn the situation around.[2]

The obvious point of the story is that only a true artist can bring out the best in something, but there is a subtext as well, that audiences need to be shown the way: they are waiting to hear what you have to say. This can feel scary, but it does not need to, for they very much want to enjoy themselves and as a result are friendly.

Let's begin by playing audience ourselves. We need to discuss something very basic—listening. Everyone loves a story, but being good at listening to a told story is no longer as automatic as it once was. Most of us are not used to relaxing and concentrating at the same time, and most of us are not used to joining with others as we listen. Movie theaters have large groups in the audience, but it is not group listening; it is parallel listening (i.e., not shared with neighbors by interacting with smiles or friendly pokes), and it requires responding to visual stimuli, not creating one's own. Rock concerts may be group listening, but the excitation level is far from calm and thoughtful.

If you are going to be a good teller you must learn how to listen well. So much of our time is spent in isolation, with electronic gadgets such as the computer on which I wrote this book, the radio in the background, and the cell phone, that some common courtesy issues need to be mentioned.

To be a good listener, first of all, one's full attention is needed with no distractions. No cell phones or side conversations.

Second, be aware that we are living in an age when one is expected to be "cool" and not show reactions. It requires conscious effort to allow oneself the luxury of reacting—while the teller *needs* to see the impact of the story to interact with the audience. If you have ever tried to hold a conversation with someone who had too much collagen injected into her face or someone hiding behind very dark glasses, you will understand how hard it is to talk with someone who does not give visual cues as to reaction. If you have ever tried to tell someone something very important to you while they are concentrating on something else, be it chopping onions for dinner or watching a football game, you will understand the storyteller's need for full attention.

Third, audience members need to keep their mouths shut. Demanding attention by asking questions spoils the group's story mood. In other words, empathy with the teller is needed. If listeners start thinking, "I would tell that much better"; "How boring"; or "I have to go meet someone, hurry up," the teller will pick it up subconsciously. In normal conversation, I have a tendency to "join" someone's speaking. It feels as if I am establishing interest in what they are saying. When listening to a story, though, I know enough to give visual cues of my attention rather than spoken ones—like smiling at something amusing or letting my eyes and eyebrows look puzzled or concerned.

Fourth, and finally, the listener must allow the words to enter. We have such a competitive society that even listening can be done competitively, competing with other audience members for the teller's attention or dismissing the teller. If something like this should happen to you as teller, just notice what is happening, shrug your shoulders and welcome the next story occasion. Know that there are some people who need to feel dominant even when being given a gift and that this need is usually based in fear. Even the best cook has days when cakes do not rise, the shells do not come off hard-boiled eggs neatly, or ungracious guests say, "my mother made it much better."

Just allow it to happen, and all will be well in the end.

Children are usually polite listeners, although some need to move around even when they are clearly following the story, and they may even vocalize: "go get them," "yeah," and so on. That is a different situation from the child who needs to gain control while he explains that his vocabulary does not yet include that particular word so you should define it for him because he is incapable of figuring it out, imagining what it could mean, or waiting until after the story for his curiosity to be satisfied. Just be aware that not every question is an unconscious need to dominate; sometimes it is necessary to understanding the story, and a teller can explain in a way that does not interrupt the story if someone mutters, "what does that mean" or if brows furrow in "huh?"

For example, to avoid problems, it behooves a storyteller to define unfamiliar words. Yes, it clearly is a good idea (and yes, that was an example—"behoove" means that it would be a good idea to do something, in this case making sure that the audience understands an idea). You want the audience both to understand what is going on and to get the flavor of the story. One can usually understand a story even if a few words are unfamiliar, and a little strangeness adds interest. In this case of "behoove," it is just an interesting-sounding word that I happen to be fond of and was in the mood to use. But sometimes a word is part of the flavor of a story. Just as a few herbs make a stew tasty, but too much can make it unpalatable, a story is not a vocabulary lesson, although a few new tasty words can be entertaining.

Just be sure that important concepts are not lost. "Gelding" is a word most people have heard, but for the benefit of those who have not, it is not cheating to say, "He rode a gelding into the mountains. It was a good horse." The fact that it was a neutered male horse is not important; the fact that it was a horse is.

Teenagers tend to be a little more troubling as an audience, for they associate listening to stories with being a child. Unless they already know you, they are going to be afraid of two things: that you will bore them and that you will treat them like children. The first thing you need to do is reassure them that you take them seriously as adults and start with something entertaining. It can be as simple as telling a funny story about another adult, telling a very brief love story, or starting with a poem that is silly but not childish. You are reassuring them with this first piece, and then both you and they can get on with what you came to tell them.

Adults are more friendly, although they can also be more critical. Most adults are still new to storytelling for adults, but there are enough who have experience now that you never know quite whom to expect, unless you are in a venue that has been hosting storytelling for some time. Don't worry about those who are critical; they are feeling insecure and need to prove something. Unlike school settings, where students are trapped, they chose to come. That's their problem.

Sometimes you will get a mixed audience. They can be the most fun for a teller, because you can see different groups responding to different aspects of the story. Adults will get some references that children miss entirely, and children will enjoy a repeated phrase and carry the adults with their enthusiasm.

Where you are telling is another major factor. I have never told in a shopping center or at a fair where people are walking by and you must seduce them into listening. Some friends who live in suburban areas with malls have told me that if there is a scheduled performance, people will come and listen as they do anywhere else, but other than advising you to keep the stories short so that those who must be somewhere will be able to listen and feel satisfied, I don't have much advice on such a venue. Certainly it is a place where there are many people, and often they are somewhat bored, or at least looking for free entertainment, so it could work very well.

If you are somewhere where there are background noises or other distractions, it really helps if you can have an accomplice in the rear to signal if there are problems with sound or other distractions going on in the background. Sometimes it is necessary to use a mike, and when the speaker is in an exposed position, it is good to have someone keeping an eye on the situation and how the equipment is working.

My recommendation is to get and use your own sound system if you work in such situations very often. They can be expensive, so try a few out before investing or talk with local artists and musicians (those using acoustic instruments, not rock musicians) or do some research on the Internet. Knowing in advance how something works makes life much easier. For example, knowing that the system loudly squeals if it is turned too high can prevent a hostile audience reaction. Likewise, knowing where the extra batteries are and how to put them in can prevent the audience leaving in impatience.

In a school classroom or a Sunday school, I like to sit and have children on the floor. The informality suits me, but there is nothing wrong with a more formal atmosphere. Often people feel that respect is owed the teller and that is lost if the audience is on the floor. It is possible that children in seats tend to walk around less, although that has not been a problem for me. It does help to be a little higher than the audience, though, sitting if they are on the floor and standing if they are sitting. You need to have authority, even in a relaxed setting. If you have ever been at a dinner telling a story informally and been interrupted by someone asking for butter, you will know what I mean.

If you have the option, it is better to have the audience in a group immediately in front of you rather than widely dispersed. This is true even if it makes a rather deep set of rows. It is hard to establish eye contact and stay connected with a group if you have to keep swinging your head from side to side and even worse to lose connection with large parts of the audience.

When you first come in, it is very important to establish eye contact and to smile. It is best if you can connect with different people in different parts of the audience. If you are nervous, connect with one person seated toward the rear who looks friendly by establishing eye contact with that person. People in the front will feel included. If you can, later connect with others in the audience, but don't try to look at each set of eyes or you will get dizzy or distract yourself from the story.

Recently I went to a concert with someone who remarked how great it was that each musician in the group had smiled. It makes a difference in how welcome the audience feels, which will make a difference in how they react to the performance. Even if the story is a serious one, you can begin with a smile. We are not talking about an artificial grin, just a simple, friendly smile. It is not just to make the audience friendly, either. A smile has an impact on the voice and how it carries. You will perform better and be easier to hear.

Remember, you are representing humankind—not just yourself—and a living, feeling humanity rather than a mediated, disconnected population. The feeling of connection with all human history makes it worth the effort and provides a real sense of pride in the value of what you are doing.

> There can be no understanding between the hands and the brain unless the heart acts as mediator.
>
> —Fritz Lang

EXERCISE

It is time to ask yourself again just what you are hoping to accomplish. Is it to entertain, to educate, to help others heal, to promote an idea from a religious background, or something else?

NOTES

1. An explanation of this saying can be found in Virginia A. Tashjian, *Three Apples Fell from Heaven: Armenian Tales Retold* (Boston: Little, Brown, 1971).

2. Stephen Larbi-Amoah is a lawyer from Ghana who happened to take my storytelling courses in 2006. He told me this version of this story as a gift and wrote it down for me this way. He did not identify the source. He also shared a quote from Kwegyir Aggrey, a famous Ghanaian educator and philosopher of the nineteenth century, that I like very much: "If you educate a man, you educate an individual, but if you educate a woman, you educate a nation."

CHAPTER 10

The Business of Storytelling

You are such a good salesman; you should be selling something worthwhile.

—Randy Pausch[1]

Whether a volunteer or a professional storyteller, one has to deal with business issues. We have already discussed the development of programs for particular audiences and the need for back-up programs. It is also important to recognize that you must take responsibility for finding out what the program entails. For example, I once was invited for "a few classes in the library" and was quite startled to find that classes had been brought in from a neighboring school and that I was being videotaped. Another time I was given a class of emotionally disturbed children without any forewarning and was later told, "we were afraid you would refuse the group." *Always* ask if there are any special circumstances you should know about. This will not prevent all upsets but at least a fair number of them, and it will prevent self-recrimination.

Just remember that a school will usually not think of telling you about what is standard operating procedure for them, even though it may create special problems for you. Will there be deaf children in the audience, and, if so, is there a signer provided for them by the school? Will that signer stand next to you and distract you or the hearing audience? Will there be a separate area for children in wheelchairs that will force you to turn back and forth while telling your story? Are there many children who are not comfortable with English and who will have trouble following your words and feel left out and resentful, or will there be a translator?

Sometimes, being given a little time to prepare can prevent problems; occasionally, you may find that some issue is beyond you and it is better to pass on the offer. If your family has just grown to include a baby with Down syndrome, you may not be emotionally ready to take on an audience with such children. Odds are you will become someone who works well with such an audience but not until you are ready. You do not want to risk your reputation as a successful teller, and what is too much for one teller may not bother another, so don't feel guilty; it will all come out in the wash.

It took me a long time to take on an auditorium, and I still don't like such a big group, although it can be exhilarating if it is a group with which you are comfortable. Remember how we talked of informal back porch tellers as opposed to formal occasion tent tellers? You may be better with a small group and give them something deeper and more personal than the entertainment provided in an auditorium. Just as there are some singers who can take on huge audiences and others who do well with small groups, so it is with tellers. Performing as a soloist at the Metropolitan Opera or at the National Storytelling Festival in Jonesboro is glamorous and wonderful but not right for all performers. Some do better in a coffeehouse. Bigger is not necessarily better.

There are additional issues in dealing with large groups or open areas, as discussed in chapter 9. There are occasions when sound equipment is needed. We have already touched on the need for planning ahead in terms of equipment but let me emphasize again that, awkward as it may be to schlep a microphone and speakers, it is much better to use your own equipment *and be familiar with it beforehand* than to struggle with equipment that does not work well or does not suit your voice or screeches just as you hit the climax of a story. If, like me, you unconsciously move your head a great deal, a floor mike is not a good choice because there will undoubtedly be someone in the back who has trouble hearing and will be disappointed and who will probably give feedback about your inadequacy. A lapel mike or headset mike will work better. Again, I do not like storytelling as a "performance art" as much as I like it as an informal, natural event, but if one is going to take it on seriously, there will be occasions where and when it becomes necessary to use sound equipment. If people are paying, they will not accept muffled sound.

The other aspect of sound that is relevant here is that of clarity. We have discussed accents elsewhere, but they are relevant in this context in terms of how easily they are understood. Offending listeners is something you want to avoid regardless of whether they are paying you or not, but being able to understand you is something paying customers have a right to demand. You must be easily understood.

I have mentioned elocution and how it has gone out of fashion, but the underlying principle of teaching people to speak to groups is something that should still be provided. It isn't taught everywhere, though, so check out local classes at a community college (music and drama departments might have them) or, again, Toastmasters might be helpful. Or a local singing teacher might be able to help. Some of us can project our voices naturally but most of us need to be taught.

Costume is a personal issue. I have occasionally worn something special but be very careful with this. Wear something that will give you confidence, not make you feel self-conscious or embarrass your audience. I have spoken of Brother Blue, one of the beloved and great American storytellers of recent memory. He wore a jester's costume and made it work, but I must admit that the first few times I saw him (before hearing him tell) I avoided him because his outfit embarrassed me. I remember when I told a friend who had been a library storyteller along with me that I was going to do my first fancy storytelling at an occasion she would attend. She said, "Oh, no, Amy. If you show up in a dirndl skirt I will disown you." She was referring to the fact that some people like to dress up in folk costume and conspicuously pose as an "artiste." Know that some people will be afraid of you as a potentially uncontrolled crazy person when you announce that you are a storyteller. Some people have doubts about any performing artist, so it is usually better to be on the safe side and soothe audiences until you are better known and in demand, at which point you can do what you want.

Once you are ready to try telling for money, a big concern is how to find audiences who are willing to pay. One of the biggest is schools, and sometimes Sunday Schools or civic associations. I have done

Sunday Schools only as a volunteer, but I understand that there are some institutions and some occasions that will pay. It is a similar situation with synagogues and presumably with other houses of worship. Sometimes hospitals and retirement centers have budgets for performances; certainly they have audiences who enjoy listening.

Shopping centers, fairs, and other gatherings often hire storytellers. If there is a local storytellers association, it may well be able to give you advice about such commercial operations and their policies. It does not hurt to contact them on your own; at worst they will say "no" or that there is a list of acceptable performers and you can find out how to get on that list.

School systems very often have budgets for performances, but it is important to understand that many systems have lists of accepted performers and you cannot be hired unless you are on that list. There are library systems that also have lists of acceptable performers. Certainly it is a good idea to find out what is involved in your local situation. You may have to be fingerprinted to be around children, you may have to audition, or you may need some kind of license. Again, a local storytellers association may well be able to give you advice.

I have told at birthday parties, weddings, and memorial services, generally for love rather than money, but there are people willing to pay. Whatever else you do, understand how important word of mouth is. It is nice to get statements that will look good on a brochure, but it is better to have someone who will tell others in similar situations about how good you are.

If you get famous, even locally, that is wonderful and you can pick and choose where you want to tell. Do not expect to be able to earn your living at it for some time, though. Most storytellers do not make a living out of it, although there are some who prosper and a few who make really good money. In other words, don't quit your day job. I say about this the same thing I say about librarianship: you don't ordinarily get paid well in money, but this means that it remains a field that does not attract those who are primarily interested in money, so you will meet and work with nice, generous people. It is a calling, not a common career path, and usually you will find people friendly and happy to share.

It is a good idea to get listed on sites like the National Storytelling Directory from the National Storytelling Network (NSN).[2] One can get a straight listing, which is not expensive, or an ad, which costs a bit more, similar to a phone book's yellow pages. You may not get a lot of calls from such a listing, but it gives you authority. There are many state and local associations, which also have listings and are worth connecting with. Look on the Internet for such groups; there are many such listed on the NSN Web site.

It is a good idea to set up a fee schedule in advance. Inexperienced tellers should not ask for too much to begin with. You do not have to publish rates but have figures in mind, preferably written down, so that you can quote them easily. Are you being asked for a single class, a series, multiple classes, or for an auditorium performance? Is it for a half hour, a half day, or a whole day? Think about traveling costs and time, as well as preparation time. Subway fare is one thing, gas and travel time for a hundred miles something else, and plane fare still another. Obviously, you need to sort it all out. For example, you should not charge the first venue for all the time it took to learn stories (unless they were specially requested, of course) but guess how many times you will tell a story before you come up with a figure. Don't price yourself out of the market, but show respect for what you are doing. It varies widely from place to place, person to person, and occasion to occasion.

I tell clients that I have a sliding scale and indeed I do. If it is a group that has little money, I charge little or nothing. Occasionally I charge quite a bit. Part of my feeling is that others are doing it for a living, and I don't want to compete with them, since I have a regular income from teaching, but I also want to support the idea that this is a profession and worthy of good pay.

Last year I had a student who, as a library trustee, had to okay paying for storytellers and thought they should be willing to tell for free. Only after she had gone through the class and seen how much work was involved did her attitude change to one of respect and willingness to pay.

There are income tax issues relating to being a freelance storyteller. On the other hand, you should be able to deduct office expenses from a room in your house if you devote it to storytelling work. If this should become a true vocation, be wise enough to find out from a tax advisor in your state what the situation is for you.

There are books with advice about various issues relating to freelancing. New York has an independent freelancers union that provides health care coverage and other types of support, and there may well be something available locally where you are.

There are several books dealing with the issues relating to professional storytelling, and they are well worth looking at. This book is not primarily concerned with professional telling, since it is aimed at beginners, but you may find it interesting to at least know what advice is available. I recommend three, all by those who know the business part of it better than I do. They include David Mooney and Bill Holt's *The Storyteller's Guide*, Harlynne Geisler's *The Storytelling Professional*, and Dianne de las Casas's *The StoryBiz Handbook*.[3] Another book that deserves to be pointed out in this context is *Who Says: Essays on Pivotal Issues in Contemporary Storytelling*.[4] This addresses many issues other than financial ones and offers a very different perspective from this book. It is important to consider many such attitudes as you form and shape your own.

One of the issues is trying out new stories, particularly ones that are original. Something I learned from Elizabeth Ellis is the value of having a "home venue" where you can try out new material. If people know you and how well you can tell, they will forgive the occasional "off day" or story that does not work, and you do not risk failing a paying audience with a story that really doesn't work. It's a little like hiring a family, which can be a good idea, since biological families can get very tired and bored at having to play audience. It can be a storytelling group, or a local school or Sunday school that knows you and enjoys listening to stories.

Remember, being paid for what you are doing is the common definition of "professional," but those who tell in a formal setting, beyond the back porch or a bar, are representing all storytellers and should take both the telling and themselves seriously and respectfully. Being a storyteller is an honor worthy of respect.

> Those who dance are considered insane by those who can't hear the music.
>
> —George Carlin

EXERCISE

Think about your motivation for getting involved in this field. (No one is judging.) It could be to get love, to give love, to teach, to save the world, to proselytize, or anything else.

NOTES

1. Randy Pausch was a teacher at Carnegie Mellon University, who produced a last lecture when he was close to death from pancreatic cancer. This was from that lecture, which I saw on television in 2007.

2. National Storytelling Network, www.storynet.org.

3. David Mooney and Bill Holt, *The Storytellers Guide* (Little Rock, AR: August House, 1996); Harlynne Geisler, *The Storytelling Professional: The Nuts and Bolts of a Working Professional* (Westport CT: Libraries Unlimited, 1997); Dianne de las Casas, *The StoryBiz Handbook: How to Manage Your Storytelling Career from the Desk to the Stage* (Westport CT: Libraries Unlimited, 2008.

4. Carol L. Birch and Melissa A. Heckler, *Who Says? Essays on Pivotal Issues in Contemporary Storytelling* (Little Rock, AR: August House, 1996).

WHY BOTHER LEARNING AND TELLING STORIES?

Storytelling versus Storycrafting

Traditional versus Current Forms

It is not the strongest of the species that survives, nor the most intel-
ligent, but the one most responsive to change.

—Charles Darwin

Just because a message may never be received does not mean it is
not worth sending.

—Segaki[1]

Times are changing rapidly, and this has an impact on storytelling.
There is a danger that the novelty of the new, currently represented by
such attention-grabbers as the Internet and computer, will distract people long enough to allow traditional telling to virtually disappear. The
kind of traditional folk tale that was honed by many tellers over many
generations largely has been replaced by the novel, which is written by
an individual, sometimes written in hopes of personal fame and fortune
rather than in the search for meaning. That novel is now being adapted
to the e-book format, and for some time it has often been converted to
film, which is usually the work of a committee.

Just as information has changed from public good to commodity,
story has for the most part shifted to commercial product. The lengthy
form of the novel allows for many good things, in its leisure, but pithy
"morals" tend to be awkward and issues tend to be explored and discussed rather than neatly resolved, as they often are in story. Entertainment is generally the primary goal of the modern novel, rather than a
by-product in a search for understanding.

As you have probably realized by now, I support telling traditional tales, for their truths transcend specific times and culture, and we live in a very isolated time that needs the experience of story sharing. If storytellers are any good, such tales work wonderfully well with modern audiences. I really urge you to get to know and to tell traditional stories.

The reality is, however, that the fashion of the moment is for telling one's own stories, both in person and online. Several students have been willing to challenge my feelings regarding the abandonment of traditional material for the personal story, and occasionally there is a really fine story produced that way. One of the first I heard from a student was about a friend who went through a very hard time. The storyteller turned the protagonist into a toad, which expressed her ambivalence toward him and his very sad story.

In class this year I heard a new version of a story told two years before. It had changed considerably and become a much more literary tale. I liked both versions, but the first one felt closer to the emotions of the moment, partly because it was told from the first person and the emotions felt more raw, while the later version, being told in the third person, felt safer and more "professional."

Family stories and group stories are good stories to tell, because they help tie the group together through shared memories. Stories of earlier generations can keep the memories alive. The point for consideration is that fully developed stories are easier to remember than loose anecdotes. They will be easier to repeat, and repetition is a major factor in remembering. Yes, people can be boring, repeating the same thing again and again, but they need not be if the telling is done well; such stories will be remembered for a lifetime if not longer. It may be that there is a real need for this in our time of overwhelming change.

Modern memories can do well as told stories. I can offer advice on individual stories, but I do not feel comfortable addressing constructing them in this book. I recommend reading Loren Niemi and Elizabeth Ellis's *Inviting the Wolf In*, Donald Davis's *Telling Your Own Stories*, and Jack Zipes's *Creative Storytelling* as good places to help you with developing personal stories, if that is your intent.[2]

We are living in a time of rapid change and often throw babies out with the bathwater, so it seems wise to hold on to traditional values and forms until we understand their significance. Hence, I advise holding on to traditional stories. At the same time, there is no point in playing Luddite and decrying new forms of story such as the personal story, which offers a modern setting with which current audiences can identify and that deal with realities of modern life without at least considering what they have to offer. If online telling formats are important in the future, they will impact straight storytelling, just as novels impacted storytelling. At the same time, online storytelling can reach new people, so we can hope that it will have at least some positive impact. All I ask is that you at least try traditional stories before assuming that they are "out of date"; there are eternal issues that are sometimes easier to see in other costume than your own.

George Gerbner, who was dean of the Annenberg School of Communication, reminds us that the one thing that no other species except humans does is tell stories, says: "Our ability to tell stories is important not only because we live by storytelling, but also because we erect a world that is constructed from the stories we hear and tell."[3]

We revere novels now, but *Don Quixote* was written when printing was still fairly new, and with it Cervantes addressed the issue of the printed story and dealt with the idea of overstimulation by the written story, suggesting that it was reading that made Don Quixote lose his grip on reality. At that time, reading, as a solitary activity, was viewed suspiciously because it seemed antisocial in comparison to storytelling. Now the novel is accepted as entertainment, and only occasionally does it try to be "art." New forms of story are bringing new issues, but the old ones remain. There are "art" films and there are commercial entertainment films, and only occasionally do they overlap.

In this era of hurried isolation, it is hard to remember how odd it once seemed to read stories silently to oneself rather than listening to them aloud. Or to remember the McGuffey readers, which were designed for practicing reading aloud, as it was assumed that much reading would be done as a social activity. Books used to be scarce, and thus it was assumed that they were to be shared. There is a modern parallel in the way that watching television started off as a family activity and has changed as multiple television sets in a home became common. As with reading novels, it has become a largely solitary activity, which makes the shared viewing of a movie appealing.

So there are several separate issues. One is that of sharing person-to-person as with storytelling, versus the solitary format of reading. The other is that of the story form versus the more modern forms developed for print, film, and the Web, and its myriad new potentialities and distractions.

Think about the story form for a minute. The told story is generally fairly short, so why do published short stories have so much more limited appeal than novels? Is it because readers like to be carried away for a longer time in a novel after having invested in getting to know the characters and setting? Is it the same impulse that has us loving sitcoms or dramas in which we get to know the characters and setting, so then we can relax the effort of learning and just relish following the plot, like hearing gossip?

Are such formats the modern equivalent of the novel series? Certainly they have the same appeal that Nancy Drew, the Hardy Boys, and the Babysitters Club have. In traditional societies, there are series stories, with the characters understood to represent various perspectives, just as with modern television series.

Take, for example, stories about Coyote. In several southwestern tribal groups, Coyote represented chaos and the upsetting of order, which occasionally brings good things, but more often brings only trouble. Today's sensibilities seem to be quite different from traditional ones and feed on the stimulation of change. One could look at it as Coyote representing technology, bringing constant change, for good and ill, in modern life.

In the current context, however, the point about Coyote is that he was known, and what he represented was also known. Many cultures had complete sets of characters in their mythic systems, representing various attributes, just as happens in modern television series. There were heroes with fatal flaws and villains who were angry, unhappy, and hungry for revenge. It is hard in today's world to understand this symbolic role of characters in traditional folklore, since modern audiences generally hear only one story in a series. That can create a serious problem for the storyteller who wants hearers to understand the context but does not want to give an anthropology lecture. If one has a printed program, such information can be included that way, but it is an awkward problem.

The issue of deepest concern to me right now is that of the storyteller performing in person. To listen as part of a group and feel the joining together of minds is a very different experience from reading.[4] The point is the freedom that it gives us from the ever-present electronic and print world. Adults are reminded and children are introduced to the concept that life can be full without hardware. So much of modern life is mediated that many young people are becoming subconsciously dependent on outside stimulation, such as video games, and do not independently develop their imaginations in the way that previous generations did. We are creating a very different world from that which created our culture, and it is worth at least trying to expose modern children (and adults) to the traditional world of story, just as it is worth exposing children who have grown up with suburbs and freeways to our national parks.

Just as there was a significant shift in the European world between the Middle Ages, which was a day of spoken word and Church authority, and the Renaissance and printing, which brought a sense of individual responsibility for reading and interpreting the Bible, so there is an equivalent change as the current world is now deposing that authority of the printed word with electronic communication, including television, the Internet, and the cell phone. Just as there was a loss of respect for the authority of the spoken word, now we are becoming cynical about the authority of the printed word. To quote Gerbner again:

> Printing helped establish the right of different classes, regions, ethnic and religious communities to tell unique stories from their own points of view. With print, the storyteller was out of view, and could no longer look at the crowd and cry: "Believe me; I know." As receivers of the story, we lost an absolute faith in the storyteller alone. The story was there, but we gained time and perspective. We could choose to say, "Yes, I've read this, and I believe, and I have faith"—or choose to reject that story in favor of another one.[5]

It's debatable whether the storyteller was ever given absolute faith, but maybe the stories were. Gerbner goes on to say:

> We know from research that by the time the children are five or six years of age—about when they first encounter the outside culture, either by going to school or by going to church or both—they have already lived in an informative, intense, ever-present televised environment in which all

the stories are told and retold but with very little variety. The same basic patterns are told in endless repetition but are disguised by what appears to be the novelty of the plot. Forget the plot—the plot is there to conceal what is really going on and to give the appearance of novelty. Look at the casting, look at the relationships, look at the fate of different social types in these stories. Whether it is news or drama or talk shows, you'll find great similarity in the basic constituents of storytelling among all these forms.

For the first time in human history, the storyteller who tells most of the stories to our children, and at the same time to our parents and grandparents, is not the church or the school. It is a small group of distant corporations with purposes of their own that have great virtues and great weaknesses. They are the storytellers that in many ways have taken over and given us a world into which our children are born and in which we all live.[6]

Gerbner wrote this in 1996, and now we are faced with Internet opinions and authorities, as well. No wonder everyone is feeling a little anxious about who, if anyone, is in charge of our world and choosing an attitude of cynicism out of self-defense. That is part of the reason that it seems good to return to storytelling, re-establishing faith in real, live, unmediated people. Humankind has not had enough time to sort through what all this mediation means. I suspect that plain exhaustion is making many of us start defending ourselves from overstimulation, whether in education, where I frequently see the impact in a lessening of respect for scholarship on the part of students, or wherever else. We just can't know yet what the consequences will be.

As an analogy, think about early chemistry. We knew that there should be elements for the entire periodic table, but many of them were not known for a few generations. That was all right, but what about the discovery of radium and other radioactive elements? Their impact, in terms of danger as well as value, was enormous. I speak as someone who was fascinated by the texture of the skin on my grandmother's chest, which looked like salami because of radiation burns of X-rays, which were done before we were aware of the dangers. It is amazing that she did not get cancer. We have been lucky that our ignorance has not caused more trouble than it has.

There is a danger in our becoming so overwhelmed by media, technology, and modern information forms (and I am very aware of the irony of writing these words on a laptop, checking references with a wireless modem). We do not know the impact of all this, although it is clear that many people are feeling very stressed, if only in trying to keep up with their e-mail.

Most of us don't ever think of Marshall McLuhan anymore, even as his predictions ring true:

> The dominant organ of sensory and social orientation in pre-alphabet societies was the ear—"hearing was believing." The phonetic alphabet forced the magic world of the ear to yield to the *neutral* world of the eye. Man was given an eye for an ear.[7]

Perhaps it makes sense that we are struggling now with the issues of what is true, as we deal with both eye and ear. His point about the *neutral* eye is no longer the case, as we have learned to "lie" with photography. It has occurred to me that this may be a major source of cynicism, as we can no longer trust our eyes.

McLuhan also said:

> Electric circuitry profoundly involves men with one another. Information pours upon us, instantaneously and continuously. As soon as information is acquired, it is very rapidly replaced by still newer information. Our electrically-configured world has forced us to move from the habit of data classification to the mode of pattern recognition. We can no longer build serially, block-by-block, step-by-step, because instant communications ensures that all factors of the environment and of experience co-exist in a state of active interplay.[8]

Remember, this was written in 1967, long before the Internet or even home computers. We are back again in an aural world, even through the computer, which started off as almost entirely visual but is now part of the broadcast media and is becoming more balanced between eye and ear.

We are just beginning to digest what has happened to society throughout the world. In terms of storytelling, beyond the difference in audience tastes and the forms that are available and competing, there are many issues that directly connect with the old-fashioned story world. For example, copyright and patent laws have international implications and may have the impact of the current intellectual equivalent of the Enclosures Act.

There is still so much of our intellectual life that is common property and so much available on the Internet that we have not really felt the impact the way ordinary people did with the Enclosures Act in England, when livestock they grazed on the village green were no longer allowed on areas enclosed by fences. People could no longer have their own cows for milking or chickens for eggs. They had to buy them from a shopkeeper, and they needed cash money to do it.

There is so much available through libraries and on the radio and television here in North America and Europe that we have not felt the loss as a loss yet, but tribal cultures feel it with their oral culture. Laws are being rewritten to protect the interests of such corporations as Disney. It's not just Mickey Mouse, which was original, but versions of traditional tales like Snow White and Cinderella that are being "enclosed." So far, one can still get traditional versions of these tales, but one can't help wondering about tales that used to be owned by all of the people in a culture. In the early days of the Web, many tribal Web sites included stories to introduce their culture, but many of these have been removed because they were being misused by Internet readers—being retold and copyrighted or being treated disrespectfully, for example, being told at times of the year when it was not appropriate. International copyright laws do not have appropriate provisions for materials held by groups such as tribes.

Going back to McLuhan:

> The invention of printing did away with anonymity, fostering ideas of literary fame and the habit of considering intellectual effort as private property. Mechanical multiples of the same text created a public—a reading public. The rising consumer-oriented culture became concerned with labels of authenticity and protection against theft and piracy. The idea of copyright—"the exclusive right to reproduce, publish, and sell the matter and form a literary or artistic work" was born.[9]

So we are dealing with three levels here: pre-printing represented by tribal culture and storytelling, print forms of story such as the novel, and now electronic forms of written and spoken word (ignoring the comics/manga, which allow for printed visual storytelling). All this affects story, whether as told story, printed story, recorded-in-sound story, or online versions.

Will there only be copyright versions of tales in the future, so that only original tales can be told? What will storytelling be like then? In the last generation, it was almost entirely folk tales that were told. Now it is a mix of traditional and personal tales.

What will storytelling be tomorrow? Will it exist? It is conceivable (although I admit to stretching a bit here) that we would be forbidden to reclaim the right to tell copyrighted versions of folk tales, just as we lost the equivalent right of walking across traditional paths on private property. Will buying an e-book (with one-time reading rights) give one telling rights?

In this era in which electronic media have become central, I believe that storytelling, as a form of entertainment, representing the past and its many ways of being human, can be not only a joy in itself, but can also counteract the numbing effect of the enormous changes that we are undergoing. Let the new forms of electronic storytelling develop as they will, but do not allow them to distract you from telling in person, as a real-life storyteller.

Remember the clown mentioned in an earlier chapter,[10] and understand that just as clowning could be done on television, it is much more effective in real life because a connection is made. Seeing myself on broadcast television convinced me of the difference, and students seeing tapes of those programs remark on how "un-alive" it seems in comparison to watching in-person in the classroom setting.

Remember also Sousa's words about music making and look at how much music is made in front parlors today. Don't allow Gerbner's "distant corporations with purposes of their own" to become the only storytellers. They have a valid place in the world, but ordinary people have a responsibility to keep their own values alive. Storytelling can not only prevent the loss of such traditional values of the past, but it can also make the journey fun for everyone as we travel into this new world we are creating.

> It is a matter of grave importance that Fairy tales should be respected. . . . Whosoever alters them to suit his own opinions, whatever they are, is guilty, to our thinking, of an act of presumption, and appropriates to himself what does not belong to him.
>
> —Charles Dickens[11]

From the moment it leaves the master's mouth, it ceases to be what the master said and becomes what the listener heard.

—Hindu saying about teachers[12]

EXERCISE

Think about any stories you remember that address major change in society, and consider them for any possible relevance to today's news issues.

NOTES

1. David Stacton, *Segaki* (New York: Pantheon, 1959). *Segaki* means "hungry ghost" and is part of Zen tradition.

2. Loren Niemi and Elizabeth Ellis, *Inviting the Wolf In: Thinking about Difficult Stories* (Little Rock, AR: August House, 2001); Donald Davis, *Telling Your Own Stories: For Family and Classroom Storytelling, Public Speaking, and Personal Journaling* (Little Rock, AR: August House, 1993); Jack Zipes, *Creative Storytelling: Building Community, Changing Lives* (New York: Routledge, 1995).

3. George Gerbner, "Fred Rogers and the Significance of Story, *Current*, May 13, 1996, http://current.org/pb/pb609g.html.

4. This is why the laugh track was invented for television, so that it could feel like a shared experience, which it once was, when there was a studio audience and families who watched together.

5. George Gerbner, "Fred Rogers."

6. George Gerbner, "Fred Rogers."

7. Marshall McLuhan and Quentin Fiore, *The Medium Is the Massage: An Inventory of Effects* (San Francisco: Hardwired, 1996), 44, italics added.

8. McLuhan and Fiore, *The Medium Is the Massage*, 62.

9. McLuhan and Fiore, *The Medium Is the Massage*, 122.

10. C. W. Metcalf and Roma Felible, *Lighten Up: Survival Skills for People under Pressure* (New York: Addison-Wesley, 1992), 35.

11. Charles Dickens, "Frauds on Fairies," in *Household Words: A Weekly Journal*, www.victorianweb.org/authors/dickens/pva/pva239.html (accessed September 24, 2010).

12. This is a saying from Hindu tradition referring to gurus, but it is true of all teaching.

CHAPTER 12

The Ethics and Psychology of Storytelling

> The evil that is in the world almost always comes of ignorance, and good intentions may do as much harm as malevolence if they lack understanding.
>
> —Albert Camus[1]

Many different disciplines have used storytelling to convey messages. There is a story from Micmac tradition that tells of a group of birds that are starving in the late winter months and can't resist hunting a bear that looks as if she still has some meat and some fat on her.[2] There is a group of seven birds, including Robin, Saw-whet Owl, a larger Owl, Blue Jay, Moosebird, Passenger Pigeon, and Chickadee, who all grouped together to go hunting, Robin with his bow and arrow and Chickadee with his cooking pot.[3] The bear wanders up into the sky, and the birds follow her. A few of the birds get discouraged and drop out of the hunt as months pass but several continue. Finally, well into autumn, they close in on Bear and shoot an arrow at her. Robin's arrow strikes home, so that even though Bear tries to fight back, she falls. Robin is so hungry that he begins to eat Bear's corpse, covering his breast with red blood and yellow fat and eating so greedily that some of that blood and fat fell onto the trees down below. The birds leave the bones out of respect, and those bones magically reappear the next year as a complete bear, so that the whole cycle can be repeated every year.

Now, from a modern perspective this is a tale that feels a little odd. From the perspective of a tribal group, however, it is a very important story. Why? Because it tells of the year's cycle in a way that is easy to remember. The same Great Bear constellation from Greek tradition is seen as a Bear in this one, and as those interested in astronomy know, that constellation appears differently in different seasons. In spring it appears to come out of the cave of Corona Borealis. It looks as if the bear is standing in the spring and summer, and then it leans and falls down just when the leaves are turning bright yellow and red. Then she hibernates again until spring, when once again she leaves the cave of Corona Borealis and begins the journey again.

This myth includes gratitude for the bear—which can feed very hungry people when it comes out of hibernation in spring and again, more generously, in fall when it has grown fat for the winter—and awe toward nature and earth's bounty that can reproduce bears again and again. More importantly, it provides an easily memorable calendar. When the astronomical figures of the Owls, Blue Jay, and Passenger Pigeon have dropped out of the procession in late summer, you had better start preparing for winter by drying food, because soon the cold weather will come and the leaves will be turning red and yellow in preparation for winter.

Today, we do not need this myth, for we have printed calendars and weather forecasts and canned and frozen food to make it through the winter, but the tale is still worth thinking about. The Greek myth of Demeter and Persephone, of a mother chasing her daughter into the afterlife to try to get the master of Hades to yield her back from death, is similar. It talks of how Persephone was allowed back to the surface of the earth, which gave her mother enough joy to blossom in spring, but when, in fall, Persephone must depart to Hades for winter, the earth becomes depressed and foliage dies down, until once again spring returns, bringing blossoms.

It is easy to be smug with our modern scientific explanations, but as I write this shortly after the horrific Haitian earthquake, it pays to remember that the earth has its own agenda. Claiming that God is punishing Haitians for not believing the "correct" religious faith, as one televangelist did, seems somehow to be forcing nature into a pattern that fits our own human cultural agenda through mythic interpretations, even in the modern world of electronic communications. We may have changed outwardly, but we are still the same beings inside as Adam and Eve or First Man and First Woman.

Each of us can only view life from our own limited perspective, although we may try to broaden that view by formal or informal education. This allows us to include at least a few perspectives: that of different times (through studying history or talking with grandparents) or different cultures (through studying anthropology or through travel) or different religions (through study to compare them).

I have always loved the statement made by the famous student and teacher of mythology Joseph Campbell, who compared his work in myth and religions to being a kind of Don Juan. As Campbell said, the fabled Don Juan sampled many women's favors but that did not give him the joy and understanding of being in a true lifetime relationship with one woman. Campbell was happily married, but felt the loss of a religious faith, so his comparison was based on personal experience.

One can do a kind of intellectual travel and experience many different points of view through story. This is not to claim that one can understand them all, but one can at least play tourist and let the subconscious get what it can from these stories.

Do you know "Sleeping Beauty"? Recently I went to a performance of the ballet version of La Belle aux Boix Dormant and thought of Charles Perrault, upon whose version the ballet is based. Perrault lived in France before the revolution and made his name through retelling folk stories in ways that would please the sophisticated people of the courts. Do you remember the courtiers who loved to dress up as shepherds and shepherdesses and go out into the country? He did something similar, taking folk stories and retelling them. There is no harm in that, but there was harm in his dismissing all the tales as being for children. He was raised by unlettered peasants who told stories to him until he was formally educated, at which time he left such "nursery tales" behind. The trouble with that was that he did not hear the stories aimed at adults and was very dismissive of storytelling while he was making his reputation by retelling some of those stories. In some ways it is similar to our current situation with film taking on traditional written novels and frequently showing disdain for the original intentions of the author.

Whatever the cause, storytelling became something viewed as childish and beneath the dignity of educated adults. It is only now that it is being rediscovered, often by those who do not understand or respect its power but want to use it to sell ideas or other products. I often get preachy about the subject, because I think it is like the landscape of the natural world that we often destroy to get what we want for us, today, with no thought for others tomorrow.

There is a deep wisdom within these stories as they have been honed through many tellers, often changing as circumstances and beliefs change, but still with the magic of unconscious belief in the world's innate goodness and hope that we will resolve current problems in the future.

It is quite possible that we are allowing our subconscious to be polluted as more of our storytelling is being done to manipulate. I am talking of teachers, preachers, and advertisers, as well as politicians and newscasters. All of this makes us more cynical out of self-defense, and that cynicism is not serving us well as a culture. It may protect the individual from being fooled, but it also protects that individual from being open to the wisdom being offered to the third brother in so many folk tales.

We are becoming a culture of first and second brothers, smart but closed to wisdom. Maybe we can use storytelling as a means of connecting with each other to keep hope alive and start some new ideas. My personal hope is that live storytelling can stay alive. We cannot reach as many as those using the media can, nor those using the Internet, which is developing its own new forms of storytelling, just as print brought the novel, but we can keep traditional person-to-person telling alive until circumstances make its strengths recognized again.

I recently saw *Invictus*, the movie in which Morgan Freeman plays Nelson Mandela, who used rugby to emotionally unite black and white South Africans. That was double storytelling. A story based in history, and the story of success that all South Africans, regardless of racial background, told themselves as they fought for the rugby World Cup. It could be viewed as a form of positive advertising to help counteract the sense of powerlessness: "I am the master of my fate, the captain of my soul."[4]

As I was working on the previous section, I had the PBS channel on, which was showing a film on the surgical procedure for dealing with cataracts. I was interested enough not to turn the television off. At the end, there was a discreet message that the program had been paid for by a Cataract Surgery Group. That made me shiver. Is that public service or advertising? It is this kind of thing that is building cynicism into our brains as self-defense.

This is why I want to keep in-person storytelling alive, particularly folk tales because they have survived many ages, through wars, plagues, and individual situations. Personal storytelling with its modern stories is very appealing, but I want to keep the old stories alive, in case there is something we need to hear to keep our basic humanity alive in the heavily mediated information transfer and entertainment of the postmodern world in which we live. There is no "evil" in the media, but this dependence on communication without live people is probably a major factor in the cynicism that is building in our society.

All that being said, I want to get back to "Sleeping Beauty," because it introduces the subconscious learning that storytelling has been so important to throughout human history, before psychology claimed to understand it all. As they approach puberty, girls often go through a stage where they become disconnected from the people they have been very close to—their family. They don't act out as often as boys do, but they seem to withdraw inside (or today, inside the world of the cell phone and e-mail). When they come out of this stage, they are ready to meet the prince and begin a new adult life. Listening to "Sleeping Beauty" and hearing about the old witch who introduced blood via the needle from the spinning wheel symbolizes the "old wives" who tell girls about the "scary" parts of being a woman, like menstruation, childbirth, and losing virginity to someone she may not even know who was chosen by her parents to be her husband somehow made the situation a little easier.

Modern life is quite different, with girls knowing the facts of life very early and knowing that they can choose their own partners or whether they marry at all. Nonetheless, they still have to go through the same subconscious stages and fears that girls of the Middle Ages did, and the old story may help that process. I remember a niece asking her mother whether she had to move away and get married when she grew up, because she wanted to stay home. Her mother told her she would be welcome to stay but would not want to when the time came. She was somewhat reassured, but the point remains that today's girls are still girls, in spite of current sophisticated culture.

Boys have their own patterns. "Jack and the Beanstalk" typifies one of those. Jack is told by his widowed mother to go sell the cow and bring back lots of money. (The cow, of course, symbolizes childhood and infancy and drinking milk from one's mother's breast.) Jack finds a man who talks him into trading the cow for a handful of "magic" beans. Needless to say, the mother who had been counting on the money to live on is very angry, and she discards the beans and sends Jack to bed without supper. The magic beans grow vines in the night (representing a boy's first erections and wet dreams—remember that the beans came from the unnamed man, representing all men, and that those beans were not respected by his mother). Jack climbs these vines, where he finds wonderful treasures: sacks of gold, a singing harp, and golden eggs or a hen that lays golden eggs. The only problem is that an ogre (representing Jack's father and other adult males of power) owns them and they must be taken from him, which is dangerous and frightening. The ogre even tries to climb down Jack's vines, and Jack must cut them down in order to survive. The story ends with Jack winning the admiration of his mother and a fine future of self-respect and comfort. Again, our modern trappings have changed, but boys still need to "cut the apron strings" and face the competitive world of men.

It is interesting to tell both these stories to mixed audiences. The girls are polite through "Jack and the Beanstalk," and the boys tolerate "Sleeping Beauty." Children too young and teenagers beyond these stages will also be polite, but it is clear that they hear the story as a story, not as a meaningful romance. Even for listeners of the right age, sophistication may demand a cool reception, but in spite of that, one can feel the response.

Other tales deal with other issues. Facing death, a husband's jealousy over a wife's attention to a baby, greed, and grieving all are themes in stories I have told. Again, the attitude that stories are just for children is quite wrong, for we all have problems to face and can find unconscious support.

I do not like to emphasize this psychological aspect of storytelling, because it could interfere with your telling, both in the telling and in your interaction with the audience, for that audience reacts unconsciously to your subconscious knowledge and attitudes. Leaving this to the subconscious is wise if you want to be a good teller. As Joseph Campbell said, being a storyteller is a different role from that of folklorist or psychologist. If you find the subject something worth following up, though, Carl Gustav Jung has written fascinating material.

In an odd way, this feels like a good way to tie together the issue of respecting the unconscious wisdom of stories and the subject of ethics. If you are an expert in the psychological aspects of storytelling, you might be a good Ericksonian therapist, but as a storyteller, you might become manipulative. Teaching through storytelling is similar. Someone recently told me that the modern American school system was designed to produce factory workers.[5] Whether that is true or not, when telling to children, let the children decide what a story means to them, don't short circuit the process by asking them to write out what it means to them, as teachers often do because they believe it makes children "think." It does, but it makes them think with the rational part of their brain, which is not what storytelling is for. Trust their subconscious minds or at least give them some healthy exercise. Storytelling has been used in many fields and is being adapted to new ones as they spring up, but it needs to remain true to its ancient roots, or like the rain forests of South America, it could disappear and leave us very much poorer. Think of the old saying, "give a man a fish and you feed him for a day, teach him how to fish and he can feed himself for a lifetime." Story does not supply answers, but it gives one principles from which to provide one's own answers. We are teaching not to a test, but to the questions of life.

I end this chapter with a story and a quote from a friend and neighbor who was raised in New York by an immigrant father from Italy who took education seriously. He didn't have money for extras, like dessert, for his children, just enough for plain food and school tuition.

> When my father finished dinner he would ask each of us what we wanted for dessert, as a kind of game. . . . I would choose watermelon, or a cannoli or ice cream, and he would draw it on a piece of paper and hand it to me. Each of us got what we wanted and enjoyed the experience.

He added that bragging about their desserts was sweeter than any sugary dish could have been. This is the value of storytelling—sharing imagination. He also gave me the following Italian proverb and its translation, which bring up the connection between aesthetics and ethics. Now I share it with you to ponder:

> *Quello che sto per divi non puo essere vero, ma il racconto e cosi bello, lo farpalcun modo.* (What I am about to tell you may not be true, but the telling is so beautiful I shall do so anyway.)[6]

EXERCISES

Think of a story you remember from somewhere and its ethical implications. What does the story suggest?

Think about a movie or television show you saw recently and its ethical implications. What does its story suggest?

NOTES

1. Albert Camus, *The Plague* (New York: Knopf, 1948).

2. This is based on a Micmac version of a tale found in many of the woodland tribes of northeastern North America. It was heard by Stansbury Hagar and published as "The Celestial Bear," *Journal of American Folklore* 13 (1900): 92–103. It has been included in many collections including: Dorcas S. Miller, *Stars of the First People: Native American Star Myths and Constellations* (Boulder, CO: Pruett, 1997; Jean Guard Monroe and Ray A. Williamson, *They Dance in the Sky: Native American Star Myths* (Boston: Houghton Mifflin, 2007).

3. The little star Alcor.

4. William Ernest Henley's "Invictus" goes:

Out of the night that covers me,
Black as the pit from pole to pole,
I thank whatever gods may be
For my unconquerable soul.
In the fell clutch of circumstance
I have not winced nor cried aloud
Under the bludgeonings of chance
My head is bloody but unbowed.
Beyond this place of wrath and tears
Looms but the Horror of the shade,
And yet the menace of the years
Finds and shall find me unafraid.
It matters not how strait the gate,
How charged with punishments the scroll,
I am the master of my fate:
I am the captain of my soul.

5. This is the equivalent of historical gossip. It was attributed to President Wilson circa 1913.

6. Ted Federici, a neighbor and friend.

CHAPTER 13

The Energy of Storytelling

We do not see things as they are, we see things as we are.

—the Talmud

I recently had a conversation with a teacher of the martial art tai chi after she heard me telling stories one evening.[1] She said that the energy of telling stories to an audience was the same chi energy used in tai chi. I have only felt it in tai chi a few times physically, while trying to learn how to do "push hands," but in telling stories to an audience, I do know how you become aware of a connection with them and respond both emotionally and physically by becoming louder or softer and feeling the emotion of the story so "loudly" that others understand it. It is not acting, but it is interpreting. I had never thought of it as a physical energy moving from person to person, but that is an interesting thought, and it has stayed with me.

What she said made me think about the energy of speaking. Whether the intent is to please people, preach to them, or convince them to buy or to vote, it is there. Thinking about the martial arts and violence made me think of Hitler and how he used talking to convince people of things that now seem evil, even to those who at the time were convinced.[2] The point I am trying to make is that any energy, whether vocal or physical, is neutral in itself; it is how it is used that makes it a force for good or bad. "Push voice" like "push hands" is based on consciousness and intent.

Before anyone turns away from all this with disgust over the un-scientific "woo-woo" tone, I want to say that it is no different from the feeling one often gets when the driver in front of you is about to change lanes without signaling. You are responding unconsciously, that is all it is, but it is an important part of any public speaking, re-gardless of the occasion.

Do not expect to "feel" anything when you tell. Few beginning sto-rytellers are going to function at an equivalent level to Julia Child's cooking expertise. That's fine; such is not anticipated. Boiling an egg, making toast and coffee, and pouring orange juice produces a delight-ful breakfast, too. It is a big step up from pouring cold cereal, but it is not yet attempting to produce crêpes suzette or perfect omelets. Don't try too much at once. In terms of storytelling, if you have a great memory, try memorizing something—but not a major epic like *Beowulf* (crêpes suzette), just a Sandburg or Kipling story (scrambled eggs) that should have appeal to an audience. If you don't feel sure of your memory, choose a story you remember from your own child-hood (boiling an egg). Or start looking in collections and see what feels right.

Getting back to the issue of energy, though, it is very important right now. You must on some level connect with the power or energy of the story. You can be a Christian, Wiccan, Muslim, Taoist, or ani-mist, telling a story from your own or another tradition to an audience of a single faith or of mixed faiths. You can be an atheist and be a fine storyteller. What you cannot be is a fake, a hypocrite, or disrespectful of the story being told, its tradition, or the audience. Cynics may do well in bars, but rarely make good tellers otherwise. Even good tall tale tellers have to have a tone that makes it clear they are sharing a "story" with you; liars are something pathological that is not relevant here, although lying is sometimes called "storytelling."

Storytelling is a good thing, but trusting that it cannot be subverted is naive. Presumably, anyone reading this is not looking to tell stories to damage society or individuals but being aware of that possibility is wise. Thinking about the role of a story and of a storyteller brings to mind the *The Zebra Storyteller*, which is introduced in the next chapter. The cat and the zebra were both storytellers, one for self-aggrandizement, the other to protect society. The problem is that the protector was so sure that he was right that it justified his getting rid of the other. I do not justify character assassination, let alone physical assassination, but "making people think" is something else. It is not just fair game, but one of the ways a storyteller (and society) "wins."

This is also a good time to point out the use of a story to demonstrate a point, which brings an issue to life in a way that straight talking doesn't always do. Business has learned this and uses it in advertising; religion uses it in parables. That point is discussed elsewhere, but it seemed appropriate to mention it in this context.

The following parable is at the beginning of Amy Tan's *Saving Fish from Drowning*:[3]

> A pious man explained to his followers: "It is evil to take lives and noble to save them. Each day I pledge to save a hundred lives. I drop my net in the lake and scoop out a hundred fishes. I place those fishes on the bank, where they flop and twirl. 'Don't be scared,' I tell those fishes. 'I am saving you from drowning.' Soon enough, the fishes grow calm and lie still. Yet, sad to say, I am always too late. The fishes expire. And because it is evil to waste anything, I take those dead fishes to market and I sell them for a good price. With the money I receive, I buy more nets so I can save more fishes."

This parable makes it clear that good intentions are not sufficient. Or one could interpret the "pious man" speaker as a conscious hypocrite, which would lead to a very different telling and very different connections. It's up to you; the story itself is ambiguous so you have your choice. Either way, one must have understanding, as well, and a mind open to new perspectives.

A related topic is that of change in attitude. The fish story deals with someone who refuses to learn from experience. The same issue is something storytellers also must deal with. As humans, we change, and a story we once told may no longer feel "right," while we may "grow" into others as we become older and—it is to be hoped—a little wiser. It may be that a story you once avoided is now something that feels comfortable, while others that were staples now feel stale. Don't waste time on regret; move on.

Here is another story talking directly about the issues of truth and honesty in terms of absolute honesty, self-honesty, and respect. Listen to your own voice telling it.

Truth Found in a Peach Pit

Once upon a time, maybe here maybe there, a thief lived. He was an orphan and had learned very well from his tutors, the other thieves, how to steal fruit or bread from the merchants. He learned well, too, and was never caught.

But things never stay the way they were, and one day he fell in love. The girl fell in love with him, too, but she was not going to get involved with a thief, so she insisted that he live an honest life somehow. Well, he agreed, but before he started his new life, he wanted to give the girl a wedding ring, and getting a ring required stealing it.

As you might guess, his concern with getting the right ring affected his attention and he got caught and was sent to jail, where he was expected to live out his days. He didn't intend that, though, so he spent all his time in that jail thinking about how to escape. It was not going to be easy, since the jailers took their jobs seriously and the walls of the jail were stone. Even when he was fed, they did not open the gates but passed food through the bars. He kept scheming, but found no answer.

Then, one day, he got the idea he needed. It happened when he got lunch: some rice a little bit of fish and a peach. The peach was delicious and made him think of the part of town where rich people lived, with big comfortable houses and gardens with peach trees. That started the idea. He wrapped the peach pit in a bit of cloth and called the jailer over.

"Please inform the head jailer that I must see the Emperor. I have a very important gift for him."

Needless to say, the guards all laughed, but, day after day, he kept at it until finally, one day, he was brought to the Emperor's court and into the presence of the Emperor himself.

He bowed very low, and said, "Your highness, I have brought you a valuable gift." With that, he handed the Emperor the bit of cloth.

Needless to say, when the Emperor opened the cloth he was very angry. "How dare you insult me with a peach pit! Not only are you a common thief, but you show no respect for your Emperor. You should be flogged."

The man spoke further, bowing still lower. "Please listen, majesty, this is a magic peach pit. It was given to me when I was much younger. When it is planted it will bear fruit of pure gold."

"Then why did you not plant it as a young man, thief!" yelled the Emperor as he glared at the disrespectful thief.

"Well, I could not," said the thief. "I dared not tell the man who had given it to me that I was a thief. He said that the pit would only yield gold for an honest person. One who had never lied, nor stolen, nor cheated anyone. For those people it would only give regular peaches. So, you see, it would have been wasted on me who would only have grown ordinary peaches. I have been waiting all these years to find the right person to give it to, and it was just as I spent time thinking in jail that I came to realize that you were the right person."

The Emperor grew redder than ever. While he was more honest than most men in such a position of power, his memory reminded him of younger days when he had occasionally told the slightest of lies and had definitely cheated others in becoming Emperor. "No, I couldn't accept it," he said. "I don't need it." He mumbled into his beard for a minute. "I think the person who should have it is my Prime Minister."

All eyes turned to the Prime Minister who was also bright red now with embarrassment. "Oh no, I am afraid that I am not the right person, either." He almost stammered, as he remembered some of the things he had done and all the bribes he had accepted from people who wished him to get the Emperor to do something. "Maybe the Head General of the Army would be a better choice."

The Head General turned red also and mumbled a little. He remembered a few people who had gotten in his way who had been taken out of it. He then suggested the Governor, who could not accept the seed, as he had gotten very wealthy through the work of peasants who had remained very poor.

Well, things went on this way through all the important officials who were in the audience hall. Finally, there was no one left in the room to take the magic seed, as each man had used his position of power to cheat or steal or kill. All kept silent.

Then, the Emperor started to smile. "You know, you are a very clever man. You have shown us how costly your crime was to you, while we go free in spite of ours. All right. Your prison sentence is done. Please return to your life as an honest man, as I hope all of us in this room will."

That was how it happened that a free man left the court with a peach pit in his pocket, where it stayed for the rest of his life, which he spent with the girl he loved. He passed it on to his children, along with the story, to remind them that honesty can yield more than gold.[4]

The point of this chapter is that one can only do one's best, but that it is required whenever one tells a story. As I write this, I am thinking of someone who has a wonderful voice and can speak very well but who does not have real integrity. Although his voice has gotten him positions of considerable responsibility, he cannot keep them. People come to sense that he is not true at heart. He can speak of ideas but not from the heart. It is living proof of the old saying, "While it is good to speak well, it is better to speak the truth."[5]

Not everything must be full-tilt pompous, but even with stories that are just for the entertainment of a good time and fun, there must be a sense of respect for the story and the listeners. Our current era's characteristic disdain and scorn may protect the speaker from being judged "stupid" or "naive," but they also prevent him from being trusted in the way a teller needs to be.

Finally, after those stories that contain warnings about integrity, I want to end on a positive note with a brief parable that was all over the Internet several years ago.

A boy was on a beach covered with starfish stranded in the hot sun after a storm brought them high up on land. He began picking up starfish and carrying them to the ocean's edge, where he threw them as hard as he could into deeper water.

Someone who was watching asked why he was bothering to do this when so few starfish could be saved and so many were lost. "What difference can you make?" was the question.

"Well, it makes a difference to the starfish that got into the deeper water," was the boy's reply as he continued working.[6]

We cannot counteract all the lies, advertisements, and half-truths that a person hears, but we can offer to those who hear us tell some self-defense training in the form of stories with their wisdom, their enjoyment, and their unconscious teaching of how to think and how to react.

If you want to tell people the truth, make them laugh, otherwise they'll kill you.

—attributed to Oscar Wilde

EXERCISES

Think about how this chapter has affected you. Did it ring true? If so, you will probably enjoy storytelling. Did it embarrass you or bore you? If so, think about why *you* want to tell stories. It doesn't mean you shouldn't, just that you need to think about it. You may just be very honest, or you might be ambivalent about performing in public.

Think how you would cast a current story in the news as a story to tell. If it were published, where would your version appear (e.g., a gossip column, on page one of the newspaper, with the cartoons, on the children's page, or as an editorial)?

NOTES

1. Carol McGonigle, July 31, 2009.

2. I feel the need to say here that tai chi is taught as a self-defense art rather than an aggressive art.

3. Amy Tan, *Saving Fish from Drowning* (New York: Putnam, 2005), vii.

4. Versions of this can be found in Chinese and Japanese traditions, and I have heard of a Jewish version with a pomegranate seed. If you are interested in another version, I suggest Robert Wyndham's *Tales the People Tell in China* (New York: Messner, 1971).

5. Tan, 174.

6. This is something that I have no source for beyond my memory of reading it on the Internet several years ago. At the time, it seemed a little "easy wisdom-ish," but now I don't feel the need to be cynical and can admit that I get the point.

CHAPTER 14

Storytelling in Times of Anxiety and Change

Storytelling can awaken a mind like love's first kiss.[1]

I have been lucky enough to make friends with a student who is of the Sufi tradition. This Muslim tradition often uses stories to make a point without preaching. As with Zen stories, these tales were intended to make one think and are full of wisdom if one is ready to hear it. If one is not ready, they often sound flat. To those who are interested, I recommend Rumi tales and also stories about the proverbial Hodja or Mulla Nasrudin.[2] One story that has always caught my attention is that of his interaction with a would-be student.

> The mullah once had a neighbor who seemed to have an aptitude for study in things beyond the everyday and offered to teach him metaphysics. The neighbor thought that would be interesting and agreed, saying, "anytime you want to come and teach me you would be welcome."
>
> The mullah understood from this that the man had misunderstood and thought that mystical wisdom came from words alone. Not long after this the neighbor called the mullah for help, since his charcoal fire was having trouble burning and the neighbor wanted him to blow on it. The mullah replied, "Sure, come on over here and you can have all of my breath you can carry away."

Regardless of one's beliefs, it is important to recognize that wisdom is more than just book learning and requires some input from the heart as well as the brain. I am trying to offer you my breath in a form you can carry. It is a lesson on the difference between talking and writing and the strengths and weaknesses of each.

There is a wonderful traditional picture from Bali of someone with his brain in his heart.[3] It appears that his eyes are in his chest, so looking at it is a little disconcerting, but the idea is important. *The heart must rule the head, not vice versa.* Not the "heart" of desire, but the heart that recognizes truth beyond provable facts and that is sometimes made uncomfortable by those truths. Glib talking is useful for many purposes, but a storyteller should represent "truth." It is possible to tell made-up, imaginative stories that are not "factual" but contain truth. Think of science fiction or ancient Irish or Scots wonder tales.

This seems an appropriate place to say that there is a significant difference between learning and wisdom. One can be unlettered and very wise indeed, or one can have a great deal of learning and not be very wise. Before literacy was common, expertise was generally gained through experience, and it taught many generations very well. Now there are many people who have had much education but have not allowed themselves to be "fertilized" by it, almost as if they attended an intellectual trade school, acquiring information rather than growing and changing.

The same is true with emotion. We have gotten caught up in the appetite for sensation without sensitivity. Modern entertainment is most often about distraction from the stress of life in order to dull the anxiety of reality. Much modern film and television is about feeling scared "safely," and that is an appetite that keeps growing, since it cannot really satisfy itself secondhand. Traditional drama had a different, sacred responsibility of allowing one to experience occurrences secondhand but they were experienced, not just observed or witnessed. As a friend put it, "classical drama used violence to horrify, now violence is used to titillate."

True drama, even today's, is taken in as an enlivening perception of reality—like using magnifying glasses that give a more in-depth look—and is shared, not just observed. It involves empathy in the original sense of "feeling with," rather than shock or pity. You have probably experienced both empathy and distancing. As the norm, we are allowing ourselves to feel things, knowing that they are not real, and it distances us from true empathy and sympathy.

On the other hand, a friend of mine whose youth in World War II Europe prevented her from being given a chance at more than basic education told me recently, "I slept real good last night, and the night before, too. My Spanish soap opera was on every night for weeks and I was so worried about them all. Now the story has come to a happy ending and I can sleep good." So maybe it is only the academicians among us who feel a difference between different forms of media or maybe it is only those of us who are lucky enough to be able to see and compare both live and broadcast stories.

Regardless of such debates, it is a good idea for you, as a soon-to-be teller, to think about who you are and what kind of tales you would be comfortable telling before going any further. Don't limit yourself, but start with something that is just challenging enough to be interesting rather than the equivalent of Mt. Everest. Do you want to tell joke stories or ones with a lesson in them or those that arouse wonder? All are good, and you can choose many different styles; just be willing to select one to start with.

All of this is to say, "welcome; anyone can play" as listener and teller, both. The more the merrier. You do not have to be great, just good enough. Some tellers will be great, some good, and some will be okay when addressing large groups, while others will be great with small, family groups on the back porch or at bedtime. Just as some gourmet chefs work well in restaurants and others only cook comfortably for a few people. Others can just heat up premade dishes: the equivalents of reading aloud. It gets the family fed—or storied—but there is no pride in the artistry of told story. People love being read to, but it is not the same. Telling a story is a bit of magic, for both teller and listener, and it connects us with humans throughout history.

Story comes in many forms, not just told story. Picture books and novels are obvious forms of story, but there are many. When I went to the ballet one day last summer, I shared a box with a retired German teacher. We made friends trying to figure out how we could each get the fullest possible view of the stage without getting in each other's way. As it ended, he commented, "It is amazing that one can still be so moved by *Romeo and Juliet*, isn't it? Having seen it dozens of times makes no difference." The story, and its expression through movement and music, is so powerful that one gets carried away with the story. The marriage of visual story and music is different from the sound of told story. Both use the ear and the imagination to create the story, but in one it is the visual aspect of the story that one creates in one's own mind and in the other we create what usually is expressed in words. Film has changed the balance between words and pictures. The visual part of storytelling has grown beyond the dance, mime, and puppets of earlier eras, and it is important to consider the impact on our imaginations of having it all done for us. I have written about that before, but wanted to bring up this thought in relation to why traditional storytelling is important.[4]

That same day, spoiling myself, I went in the evening to a performance of *South Pacific*, also at Lincoln Center, and found myself equally moved by the story on stage—remembering the first time I saw it at the movies with my family and marveling at the stagecraft with the stage rolling forward and back, and shower stalls and a stage built between two trucks (with trouble from the batteries running stage lights) morphing into Emil deBecque's estate, and then into Bali Hai. The only thing I really missed was the waterfall at Bali Hai. This time, I started a conversation with a high school girl who was really upset about the racism of this "old play" that she otherwise was enjoying. I just said, "It really was a different time, wasn't it?" so that I wouldn't short-circuit her reaction to the next act. Had she been my student, I would have talked about how hard it was to judge other eras and asked her what she thought the future would have to say about our era. That's what storytelling does: it allows us to imagine someone else's perspective.

It is important to remember that the basic issues remain regardless of the age you live in. Only you can be responsible for keeping hope up, and during World War II, there was much reason for depression and cynicism; things were pretty bad and in danger of being much worse. It is hard now to keep in mind the fact that the war could have ended very differently. Storytelling reminds us of history as well as fantasy, and both are needed. Hindsight is good for making one feel stupid (as in, "I wish I had bought a big apartment in Manhattan when I could have") or smart (like those friends who did buy apartments), but either way, historical stories remind us that change is a constant—and that even that change varies (other friends just outside the city have houses that are no longer worth what they owe on them). Assuming that the world will not continue shifting is a really dangerous idea.

There is a weird story brought to my attention by a student who had found it in her freshman English text. I have introduced it to other students and the response is really interesting; some say, "I don't get it," some get angry, and some say, "oh, that really makes you think." It is a wonderful literary story called "The Zebra Storyteller" by Spencer

Holst, which you can read on the Web.[5] It is a modern story, but short enough that it can be memorized and told.

The point in terms of this discussion is that it talks directly about the power of the storyteller, not to impact others, but to become aware of possibilities "in the air" and thus allowing us to prepare for them. In a nutshell, the plot tells of a cat who learns how to speak in the zebras' own language, and by doing so, he surprises lone zebras so that he can kill and eat them. Only one zebra was prepared when stopped by this charming cat who spoke in his own tongue:

> He took a good look at the cat, and he didn't know why, but there was something about his looks he didn't like, so he kicked him with a hoof and killed him.
>   That is the function of the storyteller.

The story disturbs me because the zebra is praised for killing the cat, and my respect for law makes me react with discomfort. I recommend looking the tale up, though, just because it makes one think, as stories sometimes should.

My own reaction is colored by the feeling that imagination is at risk in this country. Students often get angry when I say this, but *Newsweek* addressed this topic on their cover.[6] The teaser on the front cover, "Creativity in America: The Science of Innovation and How to Reignite Our Imaginations," caught my attention because it suggests that the arts are no more imaginative than science. My feeling is that science can be creative ("and some of my best friends are scientists"), but what is behind this attitude that science should control everything in our society? Hmmm. Do I sound like a zebra storyteller? In any case, the research shows that creativity scores have been "inching down" "significantly" since 1990. It does not discuss storytelling per se, but it does talk about imagining outcomes and that is something that storytelling helps to grow.

Here is another story, this one a personal story told me by someone in Ulster County.

> There was once an electrician. This electrician would stand on one leg, say, "don't do this at home" and put wires together to fix a connection. His apprentice learned from his master's example and so when he needed to fix a connection he stood on one leg, said, "don't do this at home," and put the wires together.

As the apprentice came to, in the hospital, the electrician was standing over him, saying, "I am so sorry. I thought you knew I had a wooden leg. Electricity won't go through wood, so I would just lift my flesh-and-blood leg to avoid getting shocked."

It is funny, like the Darwin Awards, except perhaps to the shocked and humiliated apprentice, who had enough luck to survive a major electric shock and enough of a sense of humor to tell the story even though it was not flattering, and he must have known it would be passed on.[7] But there is a real point to the story: listen not only to the verbal lesson, but also to what is left unsaid, what is so automatic to the teller's thinking that it doesn't occur to that teller to say it.

Our era in general, and the world of learning in particular, carries a trap—that of cynicism. My father used to tell me how he grew so smart in college that he became smugly cynical—a failing so common that the term "sophomoric," suggesting the stupidity and smugness of the know-it-all, came to describe it. Only the experiences of adult responsibility taught him that being smart isn't enough to answer all questions.

He had a student, smart—brilliant in fact—who was used to impressing everyone with his intelligence. He submitted a paper to my father that was brilliant but shallow, and he received the first B of his heretofore A career. He hated my father for years but eventually came to be grateful for the gift of honesty rather than an easy A.

Many years later, he became friends with my mother—and as a consequence, with my father—and later, through one of those odd coincidences of fate, with me, and he told me this story. My father had pointed out the difference between a flesh leg and a wooden one and given him a painful but valuable lesson. Mutual admiration is more comfortable, but true friendship and teaching require honesty, not just niceness. Sometimes stinky fertilizer is needed to make things grow.

Goodness knows that we are living in a time when honesty is not a given, and we must recognize that story is a medium that can grow many things, not just beautiful flowers, but also weeds and poison ivy. One can't help but wonder what Hitler told himself as story. It is well known that he loved the symbolic story of Wagner's Ring cycle, based on Teutonic mythology of gods and dwarfs, but what did he get from it? What other stories did he incorporate into his worldview?

What did you get from the television family shows you watched as a child? Hunger for what *The Waltons* represented and resentment that your own family didn't measure up? Did you develop cynicism about their "unreality" as a consequence?

Psychology says that we are what we think we are. Few of us have a mythic view anymore. Now the perspective is more likely to be that of a rushed sitcom with "smart-ass" rather than "wise" viewpoint. It is still possible to aim for wisdom, and even to reach it, but today there is an additional cost of feeling stupid for even attempting to be wise.

Experience and research show that it is very hard to emerge from poverty, because peers think it foolish to even try and offer obstacles rather than support in the attempt. A friend recently told me that Mother Teresa's diaries showed that she sometimes intellectually doubted God's existence, but even in these moments of doubt, she kept on "keeping on" as if he *should* be there—and to great effect—until she regained her faith. Courage does not require a sword, just the determination to keep going regardless of obstacles.

Just as wisdom is more valuable than knowledge, compassion is worth more than pity. Why? Because one is internalized and becomes who you are, rather than just who you think you should be. Possessions—including facts—can be lost, but wisdom is part of you.

I remember an acquaintance who had a stroke while working on her dissertation. She kept her wisdom, although much of her memorized fact learning was lost. Often, when I think of the difference, she comes to mind. Wisdom doesn't make you perfect—or clairvoyant about the future—but it does put you at peace with life, so that life becomes a game of skill that is neither won nor lost but played for the pleasure of playing.

Storytelling is that kind of a game. Losing rarely happens, and when it is successful, everyone wins—teller and audience alike.

EXERCISES

Think about the stories in this chapter and how they differ from folk tales. Is this a style you would be comfortable telling, or are traditional tales more your style? It is good to be comfortable with both, but not all of us are.

What about the silly comments in the chapter? Did they annoy you? If so, did you learn anything about pacing?

NOTES

1. This is my phrase, prompted by what Socrates is supposed to have said: "A mind is not a jug to fill but a fire to light," although the connection is loose.

2. *The Essential Rumi*, translated by Coleman Barks with John Moyne (San Francisco: Castle Books, 1995). Idries Shah, *The Pleasantries of the Incredible Mulla Nasrudin* (New York: Penguin, 1971). A mullah is a religious leader, and a hodja is someone who has taken a pilgrimage (or hadj) to Mecca. Many of the stories are told about either, depending on where the story is told and by whom.

3. A friend brought home a copy of the picture several years ago. Since then it has become famous through Elizabeth Gilbert's *Eat, Pray, Love: One Woman's Search for Everything across Italy, India and Indonesia* (London: Viking Penguin, 2006). I asked the friend to bring back a print for me, but now it costs five times as much.

4. Amy Spaulding, *The Wisdom of Storytelling in an Information Age* (Lanham, MD: Scarecrow Press, 2004).

5. Look for yourself at the original version from Spencer Holst, *The Zebra Storyteller* (Pine Plains, NY: Station Hill Press, 1993), www.archipelago.org/vol3-1/holst.htm (accessed July 13, 2010).

6. Po Bronson and Ashley Merryman, "The Creativity Crisis: For the First Time, Research Shows That American Creativity Is Declining," *Newsweek*, July 19, 2010, 45.

7. For any of you not aware of the Darwin Awards, they are offered posthumously to people who die as a consequence of their own mistakes. For those old enough to remember the "Little Moron" jokes, they are similar, but they are real incidents. One person, for example, put jet fuel in his car, added glider wings, and took off, only to crash and kill himself. They are called the Darwin Awards because these people have "eliminated their genes from the collective gene pool." It is a cruel but very funny and very human project. Why do we laugh so hard at such things? Is it because we are afraid and glad that this time we escaped? Is it wonder at people's imaginations but their lack of imagination in terms of imagining the dangers? It is a kind of storytelling that has been around as long as gossip.

CHAPTER 15

The Storyteller's Responsibility to the Audience

Choosing Stories You Trust

Weighing the truth with false scales.

—Zerbinetta, in *Ariadne auf Naxos*

One of the first and most important things about storytelling is that it is free form, like an amoeba. It can be used for any intent. One can tell a lie to trick someone else or to lie to oneself; likewise, one can tell a story to engender hope or to establish dominance for your own ideas. My hope is that you will tell with your hands and heart open, not with a clenched fist and closed mind.

The storyteller who presents traditional stories is one thing. The raconteur who tells about his experiences is not the same, nor is the preacher who sermonizes with stories, nor the teacher who tries to stimulate their students' thought by repeating fables. The advertiser who uses narrative stories is still something else. All are using stories to great effect, but the true storyteller is trying to be as transparent as possible to let the story hearer come to his or her own conclusions about what the story means. The others are using stories to convince the hearer of something. Some of them are great at presenting a story and some are outright liars trying to manipulate the hearer, but that is a different issue for a different book. This one is about telling to share a gift with hearers, whether it is done for free or for pay.

Jesus, Zen Buddhists, and Rumi all used stories to explain a point. Advertisers also use stories, but to persuade you to buy or do something to their advantage rather than to encourage you to grow in your thinking. The fabulist telling fables to convince the hearer is still alive, even if in a different guise. The purpose of this book is to encourage the teller of traditional stories to trust the hearers to understand the meaning for themselves.

Let me try to explain this. Many times, I have told the same story to different audiences and gotten very different responses from hearers. One heard it as being about the nature of truth, another about sticking to your word, and one startled me by saying that it was about spousal abuse. None of these responses was wrong; each was right from the perspective of that hearer, for it was what had been evoked in them. Maybe a joke would help make this point.

> There was a psychiatrist who showed a patient with strong sexual fantasies a Rorschach test. Each inkblot was described as representing something sexual: either a part of human anatomy or some aspect of the sex act. The psychiatrist asked his patient whether he thought there was significance to his response. "I should say so," said the patient. "I need to find a doctor who is not going to show me dirty pictures!"

The point is that the way hearers respond to your stories may surprise you. A Vietnam or Iraq veteran may respond very differently from what you expect. A friend of mine who told a story about someone who could not get over a loss had someone say that the story helped release her from mourning. Similarly, a few students have burst into tears after I told a story about my mother's death because their own mothers had died in a way that was not resolved. More importantly, you should be careful about what you tell, for you don't know the experience of the audience. On the other hand, the friend who had told the story of loss initially had planned to tell a different story but felt a strong urge to tell the one she did. You have to trust your feelings; just don't get carried away until you are experienced enough to discriminate. Usually it is best to stick with the original plan. That is true of much of this art. It is not something with strict rules; you must learn how to feel your way, sometimes trusting your instincts, sometimes following guidelines. You are painting a picture, not filling in a paint-by-numbers kit.

You are not responsible for your audience's reactions. I actually asked a fellow faculty member (who is a psychologist and who had been a priest) about the teller's responsibility to audience members, and he said, "you cannot be responsible for their reaction. If they are not ready to deal with something, they will react with indifference, if they are ready to respond they are responsible for getting their own support from a religious figure or therapist."[1]

This may sound self-important, and in a way it is, because having someone overreact is relatively rare. So I tell you this simply so that you will not be unprepared if someone should react emotionally. If it should happen, remember that you are responsible for making reasonable choices but not for the internal workings of your hearers. Be reasonably careful, don't tell terrifying stories to young children you don't know or stories supporting one religious tradition to people from another or cruel stories at a funeral. I once told a story about a foolish girl and realized that there was someone mentally disabled in the audience. I covered, making sure the character was "silly" rather than "stupid" so her feelings were not hurt, but it could have happened.

Having said that, go ahead and tell your stories and enjoy it. You are putting out a feast, and if someone is allergic to peanut butter, they are responsible for avoiding peanut butter cookies; you cannot be expected to be psychic.

Having discussed the value of storytelling as a kind of gift, it is necessary to bring up the other side: the use of story to negatively affect the hearer's thinking. Many times I have said that you are not responsible for the effect of your stories, but I must also point out that as storytellers, you should be aware of stories that are being used to manipulate and consider what you are telling. Rather than preach myself, I am including a few paragraphs from a student paper.[2]

Libraries store our collective memory that can serve the good of a nation in preserving and expressing a nation's cultural values. The stories contained within its walls, can include myths or tales that while not factually true, serve to unite people in a shared identity. In the United States, we have several such myths we can look up in our library, from George Washington and the chopping of the cherry tree, to Babe Ruth predicting the home run before he hit it in the 1932 World Series against the Cubs.

However, as I will show in examining the case of Nazi Germany, myth and storytelling can have a darker purpose, as they can be co-opted by political extremists to infiltrate libraries, forcing a nation's collective memory to be used to radically support a regime's new programs, or legitimize their right to power. Myth and heroes built the engine of Nazi culture. The Nazis well understood the importance of using the library to help implement and encourage a new belief system for the German people. The Nazis understood the potential power of the written word to influence people and accomplish change in a society. For the Nazis, the act of reading in and of itself was a political act not to be tolerated; they feared books and the free flow of information and learning that might be available to the public and thereby, destroying the unity and purpose of the Nazi state. As Knuth (2003)[3] writes, "to ideologues reading should be only used to further political and ideological goals, not as a valuable activity to enrich the individual and enhance the knowledge base of humanity."

That student also told a story secondhand. It came from a book by Matthew Battles, which tells a story about the stories within books.[4] In the summer of 2001, Battles was talking to his friend Andras, who had survived the vicious siege of the city of Sarajevo by the Serbs. He wanted to explain the difficulties of living through this time and told the story of another colleague who also survived that siege.

in the winter, the scholar and his wife ran out of firewood, and so began to burn their books for heat and cooking. "This forces one to think critically," Andras remembers his friend saying. "One must prioritize. First, you burn old college textbooks, which you haven't read in thirty years. Then there are the duplicates. But eventually, you're forced to make tougher choices. Who burns today: Dostoevsky or Proust?" I asked Andras if his friends had any books left when the war was over. "Oh yes," he replied, his face lit by a flickering smile. "He still had many books. Sometimes, he told me, you look at the books and just choose to go hungry."

Now, *that* is the power of stories. In this case they were novels, but still a form of story. They can be used for good or ill, depending on the intent of the person "sharing" them. This feels like telling a beloved daughter to be careful of men and boys and sexually transmitted diseases when she begins dating. Please understand that this is not intended to scare you, just to remind you that storytelling is attracting a lot of attention right now and could unintentionally invite those with less-than-pure motives.

Remember the Internet. It was designed for communication between scientists, and now, according to one piece of research, half of Internet searches (barring those for academic research) and a quarter of all Internet use is for pornography.[5] I guess dirty jokes are a kind of storytelling, too. Just don't allow yourself to get drunk on the "purity" of storytelling and blind yourself.

I want to complete this section with something a former student said. She had taken a few courses online but took most of them in a classroom. When asked about getting her degree, she said simply, "You take online courses to get a piece of paper. You show up to a classroom to get an education."[6]

I think the same applies to storytelling in person, versus through a recording or online. One is an empathic connection with a shared idea, the other can be just a transfer of plot idea from head to head. Much better than nothing, but not the "real thing."

EXERCISE

Think about some stories that you later learned to be untrue. Were they lies or did the person believe them and pass on untruths? Consider this difference in terms of storytelling.

NOTES

1. Professor Daniel Araoz of Long Island University's School of Education.

2. Timothy M. Johnson, "The Role of Libraries and Librarianship under a Totalitarian Regime: A Case Study of Nazi Germany," a paper for LIS 510-03, "Introduction to Library and Information Science," spring 2006. I asked for and received his permission to use this.

3. Rebecca Knuth, *Libricide: The Regime Sponsored Destruction of Books and Libraries in the Twentieth Century* (Westport, CT: Praeger, 2003).

4. Matthew Battles, *Library: An Unquiet History* (New York: W. W. Norton, 2003).

5. This was introduced to me by Tina Chen, a doctoral student from Taiwan who wrote a paper on the different attitudes toward pornography in different parts of the world. Pornographic sites are among those most frequently used and visited on the Internet, according to Professor Harold Thimbleby, head of computing research at Middlesex University, who reported at the British Association for the Advancement of Science's annual meeting in 1995 that half of all nonacademic searches for material on the Internet were for pornography. The pornographic pages constitute 420 million hits per year, and daily pornographic search engine requests range to 68 million or 25 percent of total search engine requests. Just to be balanced, Brian Randell has suggested on the Web that Thimbleby's research was biased. Is this part of the storytelling of academe?

6. This was said by Lauren Nichols to her father Gerald, who was interim head of Palmer School of Library and Information Science. He asked her about online courses versus courses taken in person, and he told me because she had been my student.

Part IV

FAREWELL

CHAPTER 16

Storytelling Values, the Value of Storytelling

You cannot control the cards dealt, but you can control how to play the hand. Experience is what you get when you don't get what you want. Brick walls are there to show you how much you want it, there to stop those who don't want it enough.

—Randy Pausch[1]

The moment has come for farewell and congratulations. Now you are a storyteller! As we began, let's talk about the value of storytelling in terms of helping people to develop and to hold on to values. One of the must fascinating things about humankind is that each generation establishes its own values and tries to pass them along, just as the next generation develops its own. In the "olden days" when one was shaped more by family than by media, things were more stable and new generations were more willing to follow than today, but we better be flexible enough to both withstand and adapt to all the current technological transformations. It pleases me to begin this chapter with maxims from someone who did not consider himself a storyteller. Randy Pausch was a scientist and teacher who gave a series of televised lectures while he was dying of pancreatic cancer to share what he had learned. He aimed them at anyone interested, but particularly at his own children who were far too young to understand his ideas when he died. The statements quoted are mini-stories, which you get to imagine based on the themes. By now, having been listening to and reading stories, you can probably think of at least a few that would suit each of them as partners in a program. "You cannot control the cards dealt, but you can control how to play the hand" brings to my mind all the stories about a young person sent on a quest he or she does not fully understand. For example, "The Month Brothers" would fit with this, with the heroine making friends with all the brothers and the other sister demanding what she wants; the adaptable heroine gets what she needs and her sister does not.

One of the greatest gifts someone can give to future generations is values: kindness, generosity, integrity, and the value of hard work, in particular, which can be carried on, regardless of individual situation. Inculcating this belief is what traditional stories have been so good at. The simple truth, and it is simple, is that honesty brings good fortune in the sense of being able to trust yourself. Honesty may or may not bring financial wealth, but it is in itself good fortune, for self-trust and self-liking are real luxuries, now and always. Nature and fortune tend to support you, although no guarantee is offered.

Fear-based reacting and hoarding may seem smart, but they develop a culture of mistrust in which the poor princess of our inner selves gets trapped, whether by a wicked witch, a sorcerer, or "fate," regardless of wealth. It doesn't really matter what traps us—a being or situation. One can look at this from the perspective of sociology or politics, family dynamics, or inner psychological dynamics. No matter, someone who is trying to be a loving, beautiful, responsible adult finds it difficult in coping with the realities of life. Shifting that reality of modern life into a traditional story environment: to a modern teen who is dependent on adults, the story of "Sleeping Beauty" can say, "just survive this stage, things will get better." To an adult or child, the story of "The Man in the Moon" (see chapter 7) is a good reminder that greed can result in loneliness. Again, it is not being fortunate in terms of money, for the first friend also ended up rich as a result of kindness and he was happy; it was greed that led the second friend to his isolation on the moon. The point is that being greedy and selfish is what makes the difference. It sounds bald and boring put that way, though, doesn't it? But the story works and works well, and if you know the story you are subconsciously reminded of these values every time you see the moon.

Changing the topic a little, you cannot be held responsible for how someone interprets a story, but you can be responsible about setting guidelines for yourself, for example, not telling adult stories to young children. Do you remember the discussion of the ballad of "Beth Gelert" in chapter 7? It was discussed in terms of a program about dogs and loyalty, but it could also be used in programs about human loyalty, the danger of losing your temper, stories of the middle ages, or examining ballad language. Whatever the theme, it is not appropriate for young children, because the language is difficult and it is about violence and a child being attacked. I remember being very upset by it as a six year old, because the thought of an adult being so wrong was very scary.

For that matter, using story to manipulate anyone in any way except for entertainment is wrong. We have already spoken about film and the difference of a visual medium versus a spoken one. As the movie has separated from traditional theater, it has become more consciously visual, and that visual inclination leads one to action and reaction rather than words and thought. Children (and everyone else) need to develop and keep alive the comfort with thinking, for thinking carries the power to understand what is happening and to originate a sensible response rather than an unthinking reaction. Stories give this strength by teaching the listener to think and to imagine, thus giving them the power to understand and to create wise solutions. Albert Einstein is supposed to have said, "Imagination is more important than knowledge." That makes sense to me, and I want all people to have imagination and the ability to make sensible judgments rather than just accumulate knowledge in the abstract about other people's judgments. Because I began telling stories to children, my selection of stories has been skewed to those appropriate for children, but there are also many adult stories, such as those dealing with faithfulness or unfaithfulness between man and woman; often they are negative ones warning of the danger caused by unfaithfulness. Do you remember the sultan of Arabian nights who put Scheherazade through such difficulty because of his mistrust? Or how about that old, but still terrifying, "Mr. Fox," in which a young woman visits the home of her fiancé, only to find proof that he is a murderer and thief who brings women home and kills them for their money? She can only defend herself against his smooth talking by exhibiting the finger, complete with ring, of a recently killed victim. "Mr. Fox" is a very old English tale, and one can view it as being about the dangers of getting involved with someone outside the immediate circle of known family and friends or about the fear of marrying and leaving home. It is a scary

story, and depending on the hearer's personality, she will either exter-
nalize the fear aroused by making it about "Lady Mary" or internalize it
as a kind of proof that all women should fear all men. Life is a series of
choices with consequences sometimes expected, sometimes not. It often
feels like a test with right and wrong answers that one can fail, but the
results are just consequences, which are often unexpected, regardless of
the chooser's intentions. Stories can make this feel natural rather than
"wrong." The old parable about good luck and bad luck, in which what
looks like one (e.g., the "bad luck" of a broken leg) proves to be the
other ("good luck" if that broken leg saves someone from being forced
into a losing army) is a good example of this.

The desire to feel safe makes us want to believe that there are "right"
or "wrong" answers—and sometimes there are, but often consequences
are unexpected. This makes us feel as if the world is out of control—or
at least out of our individual control, which makes it feel scary and
unsafe. Sometimes the choice is to let someone else do the work of
choosing the answers, which is often a mistake, for although it allows
one to blame another for unwanted results, underneath it all, one feels
powerless and to blame on some level. That issue of choosing answers
is supported by storytelling, sometimes just by reassuring the chooser
that consequences can't be known in advance, like the "bad luck/good
luck" parable, so that self-blame can be avoided.

Stories give one the choice to work in a laboratory of imagination to
sort out values and issues relating to trust, integrity, self-respect, and
so forth in a place where no physical danger is involved. Not to beat
a dead horse, but this is different from film, which encourages one to
take things in as they are presented, rather than inviting the hearer/
viewer to consider the issues.

The work of Bruno Bettelheim is relevant here, for he said that
children who were told tales and developed their own pictures in their
minds were able to unconsciously project themselves into the story and
could therefore use the subconscious psychological messages of the
story if and when they needed them.[2] In contrast, a book with pictures
makes it clear what that story is about, and it is clear that what is happening is to the character depicted in the pictures. The magic of storytelling, the part that lets the hearer truly identify with the characters
in the story, is lost. The entertainment is not lost, but the subconscious

nourishment is lost. You do not need to believe this "psychological stuff" in order to be a good storyteller, but if it is true, it would mean we were giving something of real value to our listeners not just in that moment of telling, but for a lifetime.

Whether or not illustrations prevent children from doing the unconscious work that they need to do in identifying with the characters, picture books are charming, and as someone who did her dissertation on picture books as well as someone who was chair of the Caldecott committee, I admit that I love picture books. Years ago, I justified using picture book versions of folk tales by presenting the pictures of several versions before reading my favorite, convincing myself that this would "fool" the unconscious into creating its own pictures. Picture books are not a good source for storytelling material, however. A good picture book uses the pictures as well as the words to tell a story; it is a partnership. This means that reciting the words alone leaves the story incomplete. More important, though, is that it is almost impossible to create your own mental images after you have seen those of a good artist. Just think of a favorite novel that was turned into a movie, and you'll realize how hard it is to create and maintain one's own images.

In my children's literature classes, I often bring three different picture book versions of Alfred Noyes's *The Highwayman* to class.[3] The Greenaway Medal–winning version illustrated by Charles Keeping is almost surrealistic with its ghostly black and white images, semihuman soldiers, and zombie-like ostler. The Charles Mikolaycak illustrations are romantic and darkly beautiful with splashes of red highlighting the black and white illustrations. In contrast, Neil Waldman's full-color illustrations are romantic like a pretty valentine. Students often do not believe that the text of all three books are identical because the illustrations are so different. These differences can be true of verbal storytelling, as well.

You want your storytelling to be *your* storytelling, which it cannot be if you are projecting someone else's interpretation, for you cannot help but project the images you know, just as you cannot help but be affected by a film's imagery as you read the book. The audience deserves your version and vision.

Storytelling is important and a great gift wherever it occurs, on a porch, in a house of worship, at the mall, or in an auditorium. If you are in a formal class, you will probably have a celebration and story fest at the conclusion of the class. If you are reading this on your own, you also deserve a celebration, so find a friendly audience, light a candle, tell your stories, then treat yourself to cake or a dinner and congratulate yourself on connecting with human history and making an offering to our human future. Congratulations, welcome to the world of storytelling, and thanks for caring. Fare thee well.

Wonder is the beginning of wisdom and storytelling adds joy as well.

EXERCISE

Go and tell stories. Enjoy it.

NOTES

1. Randy Pausch was a teacher at Carnegie Mellon University, who produced a last lecture when he was close to death from pancreatic cancer. This was from that lecture, which I saw on television in 2007.

2. Bruno Bettelheim and Karen Zelan, *On Learning to Read: The Child's Fascination with Meaning* (New York: Random House, 1981), and Bruno Bettelheim, *The Uses of Enchantment: The Meaning and Importance of Fairy Tales* (New York: Knopf, 1976).

3. Alfred Noyes, *The Highwayman*, illustrated by Charles Keeping (Oxford: Oxford University Press, 1981); Alfred Noyes, *The Highwayman*, illustrated by Charles Mikolaycak (New York: Lothrop, Lee & Shepard Books, 1983); Alfred Noyes, *The Highwayman*, illustrated by Neil Waldman (San Diego, CA: Harcourt Brace Jovanovich, 1990).

Storiography

Storytelling reveals meaning without committing the error of defining it.

—Hannah Arendt

Years ago, I was the assistant storytelling and group work specialist for the New York Public Library and worked on two editions of A List of Stories to Tell and Read Aloud. (It was up to the eighth edition in 1990.) Many thanks to the New York Public Library and Jack Martin, assistant director for public programs and lifelong learning at the New York Public Library for permission to use much of their list and the descriptions of the stories. List reproduced courtesy of The New York Public Library. © The New York Public Library, Astor, Lenox and Tilden Foundations, 1990.

A few are picture book editions, but most are in collections, which are listed in appendix B. Many libraries have a collection of classic editions. If you want your own copies, some are available free on the Internet in such places as the Gutenberg Project or for sale as reprints.

Ah Tcha the Sleeper. In Chrisman, *Shen of the Sea.*
About an orphan boy under a sleeping spell, a witch, a dragon, and the discovery of tea.
The Albahaca Plant. In Belpre, *The Tiger and the Rabbit and Other Tales.*
The lovely Pepita wins a battle of wits and the king in this lively story from Puerto Rico.

All Stories Are Anansi's. In Courlander, *The Hat-shaking Dance and Other Ashanti Tales from Ghana*. A Jamaican version by Sherlock is **From Tiger to Anansi**. In Haviland, *The Fairy Tale Treasury*.

How Anansi the spider paid the Sky God's price for all of the stories in the world.

Alligator's Sunday Suit. In Jaquith, *Bo Rabbit Smart for True*. Also in Lester, *The Knee-High Man and Other Tales* as **What Is Trouble?** with Mr. Rabbit and Mr. Bear.

Alligator loses his white Sunday suit when Bo Rabbit shows him what trouble is. An amusing story from the Gullah people.

Anansi's Hat-shaking Dance. In Courlander, *The Hat-shaking Dance and Other Ashanti Tales from Ghana*. Also in Cole, *Best-loved Folk Tales of the World*.

"If you look closely, you will see that Kwaku Anansi, the spider, has a bald head. It is said that in the old days he had hair, but that he lost it through vanity."

Anansi's Old Riding-horse. In Sherlock, *West Indian Folk-tales*.

Anansi tries to win the hand of pretty Miss Selina by embarrassing Tiger, her other suitor.

The Apple of Contentment. In Pyle, *Pepper and Salt*.

"Everybody in the world that sees the apple will long for it, but no-body in the world can pluck it but you."

Baba Yaga and the Little Girl with the Kind Heart. In Ransome, *Old Peter's Russian Tales*.

"Take care. The old woman in the hut is own sister of Baba Yaga, the bonylegged, the witch."

Baboushka and the Three Kings. Adapted from a Russian folk tale by Ruth Robbins, illustrated by Nicolas Sidjakov. An Italian version is Anne Rockwell's *Befana*.

"Come with us, Baboushka. Help us to find the Child, to offer Him gifts, and to rejoice in His birth."

Bad Luck, Good Luck. (Chinese) In Spaulding, *The Wisdom of Story-telling in an Information Age*.

How circumstances change—and change attitudes.

The Bad Wife. By Aleksandr Afanas'ev. In Yolen, *Favorite Folktales from around the World*.

A contrary wife inadvertently provides her husband with a means of making his fortune in this Russian tale.

The Baker's Dozen: A Colonial American Tale. Retold by Heather Forest. Illustrated by Susan Gaber.

"If I use just a little less butter, no one will know." A baker becomes greedy from the success of his St. Nicholas cookies.

The Bed. In Belpre, *The Tiger and the Rabbit and Other Tales*.

"But when the bed squeaked, the cat said, 'Miaow, Miaow.' The dog barked, 'Wow, Wow.' The boy said, 'Booh, Booh.'"

Bedtime Snacks. In Yep, *The Rainbow People*.

"'Just your Auntie: Dagger Claws said in a high voice. *Crunch, crunch, crunch*. Her big jaws munched on poor Auntie's bones:'" A monster story told by Chinese Americans.

Befana. *See* **Baboushka and the Three Kings**.

Better Wait Till Martin Comes. In Hamilton, *The People Could Fly*.

"The timber cat says to the other cats, says, showin' his teeth, 'What you want to do with him there?' And looks straight dead at John, too." A scary tale with a comic ending.

Billy Beg and the Bull. MacManus in Haviland, *Favorite Fairy Tales Told around the World*.

"'You're too big,' says the giant, 'for one bite, and too small for two. What will I do with you?'"

Binnorie. In Jacobs, *English Fairy Tales*.

"And there sits my sister who drowned me
By the bonny mill-dams o Binnorie."

This haunting tale was first sung by minstrels as a medieval ballad.

The Black Bull of Norroway. In Jacobs, *More English Fairy Tales*.

"The third daughter says to her mother: 'Mother, bake me a bannock and roast me a collop, for I'm going away to seek my fortune.'" English variant of **East o' the Sun and West o' the Moon.**

The Blind Men and the Elephant. Retold by Lillian Quigley. Illustrated by Janice Holland.

"To find out the whole truth we must put all the parts together." The classic fable from India.

The Boggart and the Farmer. In Colwell, *Round About and Long Ago*. Also in Chase, *Grandfather Tales* as **How Bobtail Beat the Devil**.

"'Agreed,' says the farmer. 'When I've grown the crops, which will you have, Tops or Bottoms? What grows above ground or underground?'"

Boo! Included in Crossley-Holland, *British Folk Tales*.

A very short, ominous story about a little girl staying alone for the first time in an old house.

Bouki Rents a Horse. In Courlander, *The Piece of Fire and Other Haitian Tales*. Also in Cole, *Best-loved Folk Tales of the World*.

"'Why don't you rent a horse from Mr. Toussaint?' 'Toussaint!' Bouki said. . . . 'He'll charge me even for *talking* to him!'"

The Boy Who Drew Cats. In Hearn, *Japanese Fairy Tales*. Also in Littledale, *Ghosts and Spirits of Many Lands*.

"Whenever he found himself alone, he drew cats. . . . He drew them because he could not really help it." A good Halloween story.

Brave in Spite of Himself. In Hatch, *Thirteen Danish Tales*. More traditional is **The Brave Little Tailor** in Lang (or Alderson), *Blue Fairy Book*. A brief adult variant is **Seven with One Stroke** in Shah, *The Pleasantries of the Incredible Mulla Nasrudin*.

A humorous retelling of the story known also as **Seven at One Blow** in which the tailor is a timid but lucky dreamer.

The Brave Woman and the Flying Head. In Bruchac, *Iroquois Stories*.

"'Have courage,' she whispered to her child, 'I will not let this monster catch us.'"

Bremen Town Musicians. *See* **Jack and the Robbers**.

Brer Rabbit and the Tar Baby. In Lester, *The Tales of Uncle Remus*.
Brer Rabbit is caught by his own feelings.

The Brothers Short and the Brothers Long. Gross, in Pellowski, *The Family Storytelling Handbook*.

Two sets of brothers receive an invitation, force their way through two doors, and find a beautiful little treasure box. An origami story.

Budulinek. In Fillmore, *The Shepherd's Nosegay*. Also in Haviland, *The Fairy Tale Treasury*.

Lishka, the sly old fox, promises Budulinek a ride on her tail if he will open the door. Smolichek, also in *The Shepherd's Nosegay*, is another story of a little boy who opened the door.

The Buried Moon. In Jacobs, *More English Fairy Tales*.

"But days and days passed, and the new Moon never came, and the nights were aye dark, and the Evil Things were worse than ever."

Buttercup, aka **Butterball**. In Asbjørnsen, *Norwegian Folk Tales*. Also in MacDonald, *When the Lights Go Out*.

"Here comes a great big witch, with her head under her arm, and a bag at her back."

Bye-bye. In *The Magic Orange Tree and Other Haitian Folktales*.

"All of the birds were flying from Haiti to New York. But Turtle could not go, for he had no wings."

The Calabash Man. In Finger, *Tales from Silver Lands*.

Kaikoutji the terrible, who always wears a green calabash over his face, tells his daughter's gentle suitor he must carve his likeness by dawn or die.

Cap o' Rushes. In Jacobs, *English Fairy Tales*. Chase, **Like Meat Loves Salt** in *Grandfather T* is a version from the southern United States.

"I had a daughter. And I asked her how much she loved me. And she said 'As much as fresh meat loves salt.' And I turned her from my door, for I thought she didn't love me." (Used in King Lear.)

The Cat and Mouse Keep House. In Gag, *Tales from Grimm*. A lively Haitian version, **Uncle Bouqui and Godfather Malice**. By Harold Courlander. In Sutherland, *The Scott Foresman Anthology of Children's Literature*.

"'And what did they name the little baby?' asked the mouse. 'Top-off' said the cat, just like that."

The Cat and the Parrot. In Bryant, *How to Tell Stories to Children*. Also in Clarkson, *World Folktales*.

A funny story about the cat who ate everything in his way, including "a king, a queen, his men-at-arms, and all his elephants."

The Cat on the Dovrefell. In Asbjørnsen, *East o' the Sun and West o' the Moon*.

The trolls' annual Christmas feast at Halvor's house on the Dovrefell is abruptly interrupted when a little troll mistakes a great white bear for a house cat.

The Celestial Bear. In Monroe, *They Dance in the Sky*.

A lovely Micmac tale of how the Bear in the Big Dipper marks the passing year.

The Chinese Red Riding Hood. Chang, in Minard, *Womenfolk and Fairy Tales*. A picture book version is *Lon PoPo, a Red-riding Hood Story from China*. Translated and illustrated by Ed Young.

"'Grammy,' asked Mayling, 'why is your voice so different tonight?'"

Chopsticks in Heaven.

A parable about how in Hell people starve while seated at a banquet table with chopsticks six feet long, while in Heaven people feed each other across the table. (Tell it your own way.)

The Christmas Apple. Sawyer, in Ross, *The Lost Half Hour*. Also in Bauer, *Celebrations*.

"'Will your Excellency buy a clock?' he said, trembling at his own boldness. 'I would not ask but it is Christmas and I am needing to buy happiness for some children.'"

The Christmas Spider. de Angeli, in Eaton, *Animals' Christmas*.

"To this day, on Christmas Eve, we cover the Christmas Tree with 'angel's hair' in memory of the little grey spider and his silken web."

Chunk o' Meat. In Chase, *Grandfather Tales*. A short version is **The Big Toe** in Schwartz, *Scary Stories to Tell in the Dark*. Also, Galdone and Galdone, *The Tailypo, a Ghost Story*.

"The little old boy he sat right on, kind of scared and kind of sleepy, and then he heard the gate-chain rattle. 'Where's my chunk of me-e-eat?'"

Cinderella, or the Little Glass Slipper. (French—Perrault) Translated and illustrated by Marcia Brown. A Jewish version is **The Red Slippers** in Schram, *Jewish Stories One Generation Tells Another*.

"Only a low murmur rippled over the gathering, 'How beautiful she is!'"

Clever Gretel. In de la Mare, *Tales, Told Again*. A Native American variant is **Iktome Is Invited to Dinner**. By Leonard Crow Dog. In Erdoes, *The Sound of Flutes*.

The funny tale of a cook who couldn't resist tasting her own wares.

Clever Manka. In Fillmore, *The Shepherd's Nosegay*. Also in Minard, *Womenfolk and Fairy Tales*; Clarkson, *World Folktales*; Lurie, *Clever Gretchen* (combining German and Russian elements); Martinez, *Once Upon a Time/Habia un Vez* (as **The King and the Riddle**).

"If she's as comely as she is clever, I think I'd like to marry her. Tell her to come to see me, but she must come neither by day nor by night, neither riding nor walking, neither dressed nor un-dressed."

Clinkity-Clink. In Schwartz, *More Scary Stories to Tell in the Dark*.
Wind blowing, money rattling, and a ghost calling, "Who's got my money? Whoooo? Whoooo?" bring terror to the gravedigger who has stolen two silver dollars from a dead woman's eyes.

Clown of God. *See* **The Juggler of Notre Dame**.

The Conjure Wives. Wickes, in Haviland, *North American Legends*.
Different versions in MacDonald, *When the Lights Go Out*, and Chase, *The Jack Tales* as (**Sop Doll!**)
"Once on a time, when a Halloween night came on the dark o' the moon, a lot o' old conjure wives was a-sittin' by the fire an' a-cookin' a big supper for theirselves."

The Coomacka-Tree. In Sherlock, *West Indian Folk-tales*.
How the Caribs descended from their first home, the silver moon, to polish the dull earth and make it shine.

The Cowherd and Weaving Maiden. *See* **The Milky Way**.

The Cow-tail Switch. In Courlander, *The Cow-tail Switch and Other West African Stories*. Peninnah Schram used this theme in **The Golden Watch** in *Jewish Stories One Generation Tells Another*.
"A man is not really dead until he is forgotten." How the youngest son won his father's reward.

Coyote: A Trickster Tale from the American Southwest. Retold and illustrated by Gerald McDermott.
Coyote tries to fly but ends in disaster. Zuni tale.

The Crab and the Jaguar. In Carrick, *Picture Folk-tales*. Another version is **Little Crab and His Magic Eyes** in MacDonald, *Twenty Tellable Tales*.
"Eyes, little eyes of mine! Flyaway to the blue sea, quick-quick-quick-quick-quick!"

The Crane Wife. Retold by Sumiko Yagawa. Translated by Katherine Paterson. Illustrated by Suekichi Akaba.
"'Very well then,' she said. 'I will weave one more time. But truly after this, I must never weave again.'"

The Dancing Kettle. In Uchida, *The Dancing Kettle*.
"Out popped a head on top. Then out came two arms, and finally two legs. With a ker-plunk it jumped right off the table and began to dance around the room."

The Dancing Skeleton. By Cynthia C. DeFelice. Illustrated by Robert Andrew Parker.

"'Well, you don't look fine,' said the widow. 'You look dead. Now you just get yourself back in that coffin where you belong.'" American folk tale of an ornery husband who wouldn't stay buried.

Dark, Dark, Dark. In Leach, *The Thing at the Foot of the Bed and Other Scary Tales*. Also in Tashjian, *Juba This and Juba That*.

"So I went in through the dark, dark door into a dark, dark hall."

The Daughter of the King of the Ron. In Leodhas, *Heather and Broom*.

A young Scottish nobleman falls in love with a mermaid.

Death's Godchild (El Ahijado de la Muerte). In Alegria, *The Three Wishes*.

"As he entered the Princess's room, he saw that his godmother, Death, stood at the head of the bed."

Dick Whittington and His Cat. In Reeves, *English Fables and Fairy Stories*. Also retold by Margaret Hodges in **Dick Whittington and His Cat**. Illustrated by Mélsande Potter.

"Turn again, Whittington,
Lord Mayor of London!"

Did You Feed My Cow? In Taylor, *Did You Feed My Cow?* Our verses are included in Barton, *Tell Me Another*.

Beloved call-and-response chant from African American tradition.

The Doll. In Manning-Sanders, *Gianni and the Ogre*.

"A-tishoo! The doll sneezed. What happened? The doll filled Ninetta's apron with gold coins."

The Dreaded Chenoo. In McCarty, *The Skull in the Snow*.

"Chenoos began as ordinary human beings, but as their mean natures grew, they turned into monsters." A Wakanabi Indian tale.

East o' the Sun and West o' the Moon. In Asbjørnsen, *East o' the Sun and West o' the Moon*.

"Well, all I know about him is, that he lives in the castle that lies East o' the sun and West o' the moon, and thither you'll come, late or never."

The Elephant's Child. In Kipling, *Just So Stories*.

"In the High and Far-off times the Elephant, O Best Beloved, had no trunk."

Elsie Piddock Skips in Her Sleep. In Farjeon, *Martin Pippin in the Daisy Field*. Also in Association for Childhood Education International, *Told Under the Magic Umbrella*.

Elsie Piddock's skipping rope rhyme: "Andy Spandy Sugardy Candy, French Almond Rock! Breadandbutterforyoursupper'sallyourmother'sgot."

The Emperor's New Clothes. Leyssac, in Andersen, *It's Perfectly True and Other Stories*. Also in Andersen, *Eighty Fairy Tales*.

"'But he hasn't got any clothes on!' gasped out a little child."

The Empty Pot. Retold by Demi.

A child's integrity is rewarded.

Fiddler, Play Fast, Play Faster. In Sawyer, *The Long Christmas*. Also in Fenner, *Ghosts, Ghosts, Ghosts*.

A Danse Macabre from the Isle of Man.

Finn McCool and the Giant Cucullin. In Sleigh, *North of Nowhere*. Also in Byrnes, *The King with Horse's Ears*. Also as **Clever Oonagh** in Greene, *Clever Cooks*.

"'Whisht,' said Donagh, 'there's more ways of getting the better of a man than by using your fists.'"

The Fire on the Mountain. In Courlander, *The Fire on the Mountain*. Also in Cole, *Best-loved Folk Tales of the World*.

"'I am sure a courageous man could stand naked on Mount Sululta throughout an entire night and not die of it,' Arha said."

The Fire-bird, the Horse of Power, and the Princess Vasilissa. In Ransome, *Old Peter's Russian Tales*.

"And this archer had a horse—a horse of power—such a horse as belonged to the wonderful men of long ago."

The First Shlemiel. In Singer, *Zlateh the Goat*.

What happens when Shlemiel decides to eat the "pot of poison." A humorous story for Hanukkah.

The Fisherman and His Wife. In Gag, *Tales from Grimm*.

"Manye, Manye, Timpie Tee,
Fishye, Fishye in the sea
Ilsebill my wilful wife
Does not want my way of life."

The Fishermen. In Courlander, *The Piece of Fire*. Another fisherman outsmarted by his clever partner is **Anansi's Fishing Expedition** in Courlander, *The Cow-tail Switch and Other West African Stories*.

"'Just a minute,' Bouki said, 'No one appointed you the strongest. I will do the rowing.'"

The Flea. Sawyer, in Haviland, *Favorite Fairy Tales Told in Spain*. Also in Johnson, *Anthology of Children's Literature*.

"Belita—Felipa—they dance well together—

Belita—Felipa; now answer me whether

You know this Felipa—this animalita

If you answer right, then you marry Belita."

The Fool of the World and the Flying Ship. In Ransome, *Old Peter's Russian Tales*. Also in **The Fool of the World and the Flying Ship: A Russian Tale**. Illustrated by Uri Shulevitz. A shorter American version is **Hardy Hardhead** in Chase, *The Jack Tales*.

The ancient old man says to the Fool, "Sit you down in it, and fly off whither you want to go. But be sure on the way to give a lift to everyone you meet."

The Foolish Lad. In Hatch, *Thirteen Danish Tales*.

"The boy trudged along till he reached a large rock. This he thought was the town, so he said, 'would you like to buy some butter?'"

The Foolish Man. In Tashjian, *Once There Was and Was Not*. Also in Clarkson, *World Folktales*.

"I have no time to dig up a pot of gold. God has given me the Gift of Luck. I must hurry and search for it."

The Forest Bride. In Fillmore, *The Shepherd's Nosegay*. Also in Cole, *Best-loved Folk Tales of the World*.

"Take my word for it, Viekko, you could do much worse than have me for a sweetheart! Even if I am only a mouse I can love you and be true to you."

Forever Mountain. *See* **Three Strong Women**.

The Freedom Bird. In Holt, *Ready-to-tell Tales*.

A hunter is bedeviled by a laughing bird.

The Frog Prince. In Gag, *Tales from Grimm*. For the traditional ending consider Lore Segal's translation, **The Frog King, or Iron Hans**, in *The Juniper Tree*.

"Youngest daughter of the King,
Open the door for me!"

From Tiger to Anansi. *See* **All Stories Are Anansi's**.

Frost. In Ransome, *Old Peter's Russian Tale*.

In the deep, cold, and snowy woods, a kind girl and her mean stepsisters take turns waiting for Frost to be their bridegroom.

Fulfilled: A Legend of Christmas Eve. In Bryant, *How to Tell Stories to Children*. Also in Haviland, *Favorite Fairy Tales Told in Denmark*.

Two travelers, given shelter on Christmas Eve, bring prosperity to the poor farm couple who have shared with them.

The Giant Who Had No Heart in His Body. In Asbjørsen, *East o' the Sun and West o' the Moon*.

"Far, far away in a lake lies an island; on that island stands a church; in that church is a well; in that well swims a duck; in that duck there is an egg; and in that egg lies my heart."

The Gingerbread Boy. In Bryant, *How to Tell Stories to Children*. Also in Haviland, *The Fairy Tale Treasury*.

"Run! run! as fast as you can! You can't catch me. I'm the Gingerbread Man!"

The Girl Who Was Not Satisfied with Simple Things. In Bruchac, *Iroquois Stories*. An eerie, longer retelling is **The Girl Who Married a Ghost**, Curtis, in Bierhorst, *The Girl Who Married a Ghost*.

A brave girl learns a lesson and gains power after she realizes the bridegroom she has accepted is a great horned serpent.

Girl with a Wooden Bowl. In Hearn, *Gleanings*.

An orphan is warned to wear a wooden bowl to hide her beauty. After many hardships, she is chosen by the lord's son.

The Girl without Hands or **The Girl with Silver Hands**. In Manheim, *Grimm's Tales for Young and Old*.

A girl is traded to the devil by her unwitting father and is married to a prince who also is fooled by the devil. Only an angel manages to sort the situation out after much sorrow.

The Gluttonous Wife. In Belpre, *The Tiger and the Rabbit and Other Tales*. Also as **The Greedy Wife**.

The Goat Well. In Courlander, *The Fire on the Mountain and Other Ethiopian Stories*. Also in Johnson, *Anthology of Children's Literature*.

"Every night you throw a pair of goat's horns into the well, and in the morning you find a goat."

The Golden Arm. In Jacobs, *English Fairy Tales*. Mark Twain's advice on telling this "jump" story is included in Clarkson, *World Folktales*.

A ghost story that ends with a good scare—and then laughter.

The Golden Goose. Crane, in Grimm, *Household Stories from the Collection of the Brothers Grimm*.

"No sooner had they touched the sexton than they had to follow on too; and now there were seven following the Simpleton and the goose."

The Golden Touch. In Hawthorne, *Wonderbook for Girls and Boys*.

King Midas's daughter is turned to gold, because of her father's wish for the golden touch.

Goldilocks. *See* **The Three Bears**.

Gone Is Gone. Gag, in Haviland, *The Fairy Tale Treasury*. Also in Lurie, *Clever Gretchen*.

The story of a man who wanted to do the housework.

The Grateful Statues. Included in Sakade, *Little One Inch and Other Japanese Children's Favorite Stories*. Also as **New Year's Hats for the Statues**, in Uchida, *The Sea of Gold*.

"It's better to do a kind thing like that than to have all the rice-cakes in the world. We'll get along without any rice-cakes for New Year's."

The Great Bear. In Jablow and Withers, *Man in the Moon*.

Seven Magical Mongolian Brothers fight back against an evil khan and become the stars of the Great Bear. From the Ordos people.

Greedy Mariani. In Carter, *Greedy*. Also in Cole, *Best-loved Folk Tales of the World*.

She was a miser, a witch, a thief who got what she deserved when she met a zombie.

The Greedy Wife, in Durell, *The Diane Goode Book of American Folk Tales and Songs*.

This is a Puerto Rican tale of a wife who always eats all the food when her husband goes off to work.

Gudbrand of the Hillside. In Asbjørnsen, *Norwegian Folk Tales*.

He and his wife lived so happily together that whatever the husband did, the wife thought it so well done that it could never be done better.

A Guest for Halil. In Kelsey, *Once the Hodja*.
"Surely you wish the coat to eat. . . . It was the coat, not me, that you invited to your banquet."

The Gunniwolf. Retold by Wilhelmina Harper. Illustrated by William Wiesner. This American Little Red Riding Hood story can also be found as **The Gunny Wolf**, in MacDonald's *Twenty Tellable Tales*. An African American version is "A Wolf and Little Daughter," in Hamilton's *The People Could Fly*.
"The Gunniwolf woke up! Away he ran: hunker-cha, hunker-cha, hunkercha, hunker-cha."

Hafiz, the Stone-cutter. In Shedlock, *Art of the Story-teller*.
"Sun was stronger than the King, Cloud was stronger than the Sun, Rock was stronger than the Cloud, but I, Hafiz, was stronger than all."

The Handsome Prince. In Schimmel, *Just Enough to Make a Story*.
A spoiled prince kisses an unwilling shepherdess with surprising results. A story using origami.

Hansel and Gretel. Included in Gag, *Tales from Grimm*.
"The Old One called and cried, and frizzled and fried, but no one heard. That was the end of her, and who cares?"

The Hare and the Hedgehog. In de la Mare, *Tales Told Again*.
"'Heavens! husband,' Mrs. Hedgehog cried, 'are you daft? Are you gone crazy? You! Run a race with a hare!'" Aesop's fable retold. Hare loses again in Galdone's *Hare and the Tortoise*.

Henny Penny. Retold and illustrated by Paul Galdone.
"'Goodness gracious me!' said Henny Penny. 'The sky is falling! I must go and tell the king.'"

Here We Go! In Leach, *The Thing at the Foot of the Bed*.
The antics of a mischievous boggart drive a farm family to distraction in this humorous tale from England.

Hiç! Hiç! Hiç! *See* **Soap, Soap, Soap**.

The Hobyahs. In Jacobs, *More English Fairy Tales*.
"And one night the Hobyahs came and said, 'Hobyah! Hobyah! Hobyah! Tear down the hempstalks, eat up the old man and woman, and carry off the little girl!'"

The Hodja's Coat. In Spaulding, *The Wisdom of Storytelling in an Information Age*.
Who was invited to dinner? Hodja or his coat?

The Holy Night. Lagerlöf, in Eaton, *The Animals' Christmas*. Also in Harper, *Merry Christmas to You*.

A quiet, moving story of Joseph's search for coals to warm Mary and the Child on the first Christmas Eve.

The Horned Woman. In Baker, *The Talking Tree*. Also in Jacobs, *Celtic Fairy Tales*.

"Strange to hear and frightful to look upon were these twelve omen, with their horns and their wheels."

How Boots Befooled the King. In Pyle, *The Wonder Clock*.

"'Sh-h-h-h-h!' said Boots, 'I am not to be talked to now. This is a wisdom-sack, and I am learning wisdom as fast as a drake can eat peas.'"

How Coyote Stole Fire. In Robinson, *Coyote the Trickster*. Also in Haviland, *North American Legends*.

"Frog flung the fire on to Wood. And Wood swallowed it."

How Pa Learned to Grow Hot Peppers. In Credle, *Tall Tales from the High Hills*.

The granny-witch over at Bat Cave knew that "It takes a hot-tempered man to raise hot peppers." A humorous tale from the Blue Ridge Mountains.

How the Camel Got His Hump. In Kipling, *Just So Stories*.

"And the Camel said 'Humph!' again; but no sooner had he said it than he saw his back, that he was so proud of puffing up and puffing up into a great big lolloping humph."

How the Rhinoceros Got His Skin. In Kipling, *Just So Stories*.

"There came down to the beach from the Altogether Uninhabited Interior one Rhinoceros with a horn on his nose, two piggy eyes, and few manners."

How the Stars Fell into the Sky: A Navaho Legend. Retold by Jerrie Oughton. Illustrated by Lisa Desimini. A different version is in Garcia, *Coyote and the Sky: How the Sun Moon and Stars Began*. Illustrated by Victoria Pringle.

A beautiful creation legend from Navaho Medicine Man Hosteen Klah about how Coyote damaged First Woman's attempts to make the world's rules easy to understand and follow.

How the Whale Got His Throat. In Kipling, *Just So Stories*.

"And he swallowed the shipwrecked Mariner, and the raft he was sitting on, and his blue canvas breeches, and the suspenders (which you must not forget), *and* the jackknife."

The Huckabuck Family and How They Raised Pop Corn in Nebraska and Quit and Came Back. In Sandburg, *Rootabaga*.

"In one corner of the corn-crib . . . she had a secret, a big, round squash, a fat, yellow squash, a rich squash all spotted with spots of gold."

Hungry Spider and the Turtle. In Courlander, *The Cow-tail Switch and Other West African Stories*.

"Turtle looked in the dish. Everything was gone. Even the smell was gone." An African version of the fable whose moral is "one bad turn deserves another."

I'm Coming Up the Stairs. In Leach, *Whistle in the Graveyard*.

"'Tilly, I'm on the third step. . . .

Tilly, I'm on the fourth step.'"

I'm Tipingee, She's Tipingee, We're Tipingee, Too. In Wolkstein, *The Magic Orange Tree*.

"Tomorrow I will send my stepdaughter to the well at noon for water . . . call her by her name, Tipingee, and she will come to you. Then you can take her."

It Could Always Be Worse: A Yiddish Folktale. Retold and illustrated by Margot Zemach.

"The Rabbi listened and thought. At last he said, 'Go home now, my poor unfortunate man, and let the animals out of your hut.'"

Jack and the Beanstalk. In Jacobs, *English Fairy Tales*. A good shortened version is in Rockwell, *Puss in Boots and Other Stories*.

"Fee-fi-fo-fum,

I smell the blood of an Englishman,

Be he alive, or be he dead

I'll have his bones to grind my bread."

Jack and the Robbers. Included in Chase, *The Jack Tales*.

The Appalachian version of **The Musicians of Bremen.**

Johnny Appleseed. Blair, in Haviland, *North American Legends*.

"Then he'd start tromping westwards, carrying seed packets of one kind and another along with him."

Jorinda and Joringel. In Gag, *More Tales from Grimm*.

"In the midst of her song she changed into a singing nightingale with a beautiful red ring around her throat."

Juan Bobo and the Queen's Necklace: A Puerto Rican Folk Tale. Retold by Pura Belpre. Illustrated by Christine Price. A similar story of an unlikely detective is **Doctor and Detective, Too**, in Hatch, *Thirteen*

Danish Tales. **The Unwilling Magician** is a Tibetan version in Timpanelli, *Tales from the Roof of the World*.

"'Ay, Juan,' said his mother, . . . 'What makes you think, that you, a bobo, will find it, when all the others, who weren't bobos, failed?'"

The Juggler of Notre Dame. In Sawyer, *The Way of the Storyteller*. Also in de Paola, **The Clown of God**.

An old juggler's final performance for the Holy Child brings a Christmas miracle.

Just Rewards or Who Is That Man in the Moon and What's He Doing Up There Anyway? Steve Sanfield. Illustrated by Emily Lasker.

A modern version of an old Chinese tale about how a greedy man ended up on the moon.

Just Say Hiç! *See* **Soap, Soap, Soap!**

Kantchil's Lime Pit. In Courlander, *Kantchil's Lime Pit and Other Stories from Indonesia*.

Clever mouse deer tricks the other animals into throwing him out of a deep hole.

Kate Crackernuts. In Lurie, *Clever Gretchen*. Original, longer version in Jacobs, *English Fairy Tales*.

"And this time, when Ann lifted the lid off the pot, off jumped her own pretty head, and on jumped a sheep's head in its place."

The King and the Riddle. *See* **Clever Manka**.

The King and the Shirt. In Tolstoy, *The Lion and the Puppy*. An Italian version is **The Happy Man's Shirt**, in Yolen, *Favorite Folktales from around the World*.

"If a happy man can be found, the shirt taken from his back and put upon the King, the King will recover."

The King o' the Cats. In Jacobs, *More English Fairy Tales*.

A deceptively simple story that can be chillingly eerie.

King Thrushbeard. Crane, in Grimm, *Household Stories from the Collection of the Brothers Grimm*.

"The princess was horrified; but the king said, 'I took an oath to give you to the first beggar that came, and so it must be done.'"

The King Who Was a Gentleman. In MacManus, *Hibernian Nights*.

And he said to himself, "I'll make the King say 'You're a liar' yet or I'll perish!"

The King with Horse's Ears. In Burns, *The King with Horse's Ears and Other Irish Fairy Tales*.

A king whispers his secret, which does not remain a secret.

The King with the Terrible Temper. In Tashjian, *With a Deep Sea Smile*.

"The eldest was very fat (Ka-plunk); the second was exceedingly thin (Whistle); but the youngest was very beautiful (A-a-ahh)." An audience participation story.

The Knee-high Man. In Durell, *The Diane Goode Book of American Folk Tales and Songs*.

"So he goes to see Brer Bull, and he say, 'Brer Bull, I come to ask you to tell me how to get big like you is.'"

The Lad Who Went to the North Wind. In Asbjørnsen, *East o' the Sun, West o' the Moon*.

"Cloth, spread yourself. . . ." "Ram, ram! make money!" "Stick, stick! lay on!"

The Lass That Couldn't Be Frighted. In Leodhas, *Heather and Broom*.

"'Hoots! Toots! to your goblin!' the lass shouted back at him. 'I'll grind my grain, goblin or no goblin!'"

The Lass Who Went Out at the Cry of Dawn. In Leodhas, *Thistle and Thyme*. Also in Minard, *Womenfolk and Fairy Tales*.

"'I'd like my older sister' said she. 'For I hear you've brought her here.'" A brave girl triumphs over an evil wizard.

Lazy Jack. In Jacobs, *English Fairy Tales*. Another boy who follows directions whether they apply or not is **Silly Saburo**, in Sakade, *Little One Inch*.

"'You ninney-hammer,' said she to her son, 'you should have carried it on your shoulder.' 'I'll do so another time,' replied Jack."

Lazy Keloglan and the Sultan's Daughter. In Walker, *A Treasury of Turkish Folktales for Children*.

"Now, the sultan had a daughter who was very beautiful except for one feature: her head had not a single hair on it."

The Lazy One. In Pridham, *A Gift from the Heart*. An Armenian version is **The Lazy Man**, in Tashjian, *Three Apples Fell from Heaven*.

"But you can't do that! You can't bury someone who is alive! Who told you to do such a crazy thing?"

Li Chi and the Serpent. In Sherman, *Told Tales*. Also in Roberts, *Chinese Fairy Tales and Fantasies*.

A brave young Chinese girl faces a dragon.

The Liar's Contest. In Courlander, *The Hat-shaking Dance and Other Ashanti Tales from Ghana*.

"Let us make a bargain. You may tell me a fantastic story. If I say I don't believe it, you may eat me."

Like Meat Loves Salt. *See* **Cap o' Rushes**.

The Lion and the Rabbit. Forest, in Miller, *Joining In*.

A clever rabbit escapes from becoming the dinner of a ferocious lion. The audience provides the echo.

The Lion Hunt. In Tashjian, *Juba This and Juba That*.

A Halloween version of this favorite participation story is **Let's Go on a Ghost Hunt**, in MacDonald, *When the Lights Go Out*.

Little Eight John. In Hamilton, *The People Could Fly*.

A rotten little child, who brings his family troubles and giggles and grins about it, gets what he deserves when Old Bloody Bones comes to call.

Little Half-chick. In Gonzalez, *Señor Cat's Romance*.

An old Spanish story about the chick on the weather vane.

The Little Old Lady Who Was Not Afraid of Anything. Linda Williams. Illustrated by Megan Lloyd.

"But behind her she could hear . . .

Two shoes go CLOMP, CLOMP,

One pair of pants go WIGGLE, WIGGLE,

One shirt go SHAKE, SHAKE."

Good for Halloween programs for young children.

The Little Red Hen and the Grain of Wheat. Bryant, in Haviland, *The Fairy Tale Treasury*.

"'The wheat is ripe,' said the Little Red Hen. 'Who will cut the wheat?'

'Not I,' said the Duck.

'Not I,' said the Cat.

'Not I,' said the Dog."

Little Red Riding Hood. Perrault, in Haviland, *The Fairy Tale Treasury*.

"Grandmamma, what great arms you have." "All the better to hug you with, my dear."

The Little Rooster and the Turkish Sultan. In Ross, *The Lost Half Hour*. Included in the novel *The Good Master*, by Kate Seredy. Mac-Donald's audience participation version for younger children is in *Twenty Tellable Tales*.

> "Come, my empty stomach, come my empty stomach, eat up all the bees."

Little Scar Face. Wilson, in Association for Childhood Education International, *Told under the Green Umbrella*. A retelling for an older audience is **The Indian Cinderella**, in Haviland, *North American Legends*. Also in Bruchac, *Iroquois Stories*, as **Wife of the Thunderer**.

> "He is invisible; no one can see him who is not gentle and good. Therefore, if any maiden can see him, he will have her for his wife."
> An Algonquin tale.

Little Sister and the Month Brothers. Retold by Beatrice Schenk de Regniers. Illustrated by Margot Tomes.

> A young girl is sent out in the winter for summer fruit.

The Living Kuan-yin. In Kendall, *Sweet and Sour*.

> An unselfish traveler is rewarded when he sacrifices his own question to help those he meets on the road.

Lon Po Po. *See* **The Chinese Red Riding Hood**.

The Lost Horse. In Yolen, *Favorite Folktales from around the World*.

> "Everyone tried to console him, but his father said, 'What makes you so sure this isn't a blessing?'" A Chinese tale.

The Magic Brocade. In Cole, *Best-loved Folk Tales of the World*.

> "Suddenly the silken threads trembled and the picture burst into life."

The Magic Porridge Pot. Called **The Sweet Porridge** in Gag, *More Tales from Grimm*. A popular modern version is **Strega Nona**. Retold and illustrated by Tomie de Paola.

> A girl gets a magic pot from a woman and the secret word to get it cooking—and the one to stop it.
> Strega Nona's magic words are:
> "Bubble, bubble, pasta pot.
> Boil me some pasta, nice and hot."

The Magician. By Uri Shulevitz.

> How the Prophet Elijah brought a Passover feast to a poor old couple. An illustrated adaptation of an L. L. Peretz Yiddish tale.

Mary Culhane and the Dead Man. In Bang, *The Goblins Giggle*.
"'Walk on, Mary Culhane,' said the corpse."
Master of All Masters. In Jacobs, *English Fairy Tales*.
"Master of all masters, get out of your barnacle and put on your squibs and crackers."
A Matter of Brogues. In Sawyer, *The Way of the Storyteller*.
"With the finishing of the song, the wee brogues walked themselves off the shelf and made straight for the door!"
The Men Who Made a Lion. In Forest, *Wisdom Tales*.
They can, but what happens if they do?
Mighty Mikko. In Fillmore, *The Shepherd's Nosegay*. Also in Clarkson, *World Folktales*.
"I fear your Majesty's wardrobe doesn't contain the kind of clothes my master is accustomed to." A Puss-in-Boots variant from Finland.
The Milky Way. In Lin, *The Milky Way and other Chinese Folk Tales*.
Also **The Cowherd and the Sky Maiden**, in Yip, *Chinese Children's Favorite Stories*.
A boy falls for an immortal girl, but angry gods separate them.
The Milky Way. In Joseph Bruchac and Gayle Ross. *The Story of the Milky Way: A Cherokee Tale*. Illustrated by Virginia Stroud.
A spirit dog spilling stolen cornmeal creates the Milky Way.
The Mill That Grinds at the Bottom of the Sea. In Asbjørnsen, *Norwegian Folk Tales*.
"And there sits the mill at the bottom of the sea, grinding away to this very day. And *that* is why the sea is salt!"
The Miller, the Boy and the Donkey. Bedrick, in Reeves, *Fables from Aesop*.
"Then with the donkey swinging upside down between them, the miller and his son made their way into the town."
Millions of Cats. By Wanda Gag.
"Cats here, cats there,
Cats and kittens everywhere."
A modern story that has the humor and quality of an old folk tale.
The Mixed-Up Feet and the Silly Bridegroom. In Singer, *Zlateh the Goat and Other Stories*.
How the wise men of Chelm solve the problems of a silly girl and her equally silly fiancé.

Molly Whuppie. In Jacobs, *English Fairy Tales*.

"After that the king says to Molly: 'Molly, you are a clever girl, but if you would do better yet, and steal the giant's ring that he wears on his finger, I will give you my youngest son for yourself.'"

Momotaro or the Peach Boy. Hearn, in Cole, *Best-loved Folk Tales of the World*.

"All of a sudden the peach burst in two and there was no stone to it, but a fine boy baby where the stone should have been."

Money from the Sky. In Kelsey, *Once the Hodja*.

"You tossed it? No indeed! The money bag was a gift from Allah. It fell directly from heaven in answer to my prayer."

The Monkey and the Crocodile. Babbitt, in Yolen, *Favorite Folktales from around the World*.

"'I wish you had told me you wanted my heart,' said the monkey. 'Then I might have brought it with me.'"

Mother Holle. In Gag, *More Tales from Grimm*.

"'Stand in this doorway,' said Mother Holle, and as the girl did so, a shower of golden rain fell down upon her."

Mr. Fox. In Jacobs, *English Fairy Tales*.

"But Lady Mary was a brave one, she was, and she opened the door, and what do you think she saw? Why, bodies and skeletons of beautiful young ladies all stained with blood."

Mr. Miacca. In Jacobs, *English Fairy Tales*.

"Then Tommy Grimes said to Mrs. Miacca, 'Does Mr. Miacca always have little boys for supper?'"

Mr. Rabbit and Mr. Bear. In Lester, *The Knee-High Man and Other Tales*.

"He had never tasted such delicious, scrumptious, crispy, luscious, delectable, exquisite, ambrosial, nectareous, yummy lettuce in aaaaaaall of his life."

Musakalala, The Talking Skull. *See* **The Singing Tortoise**.

The Musicians of Bremen. In Gag, *Tales from Grimm*. Also in Rockwell, *The Three Sillies*. *See also* **Jack and the Robbers**.

A group of animals scare off robbers with their song.

My Mother Is the Most Beautiful Woman in the World. Becky Reyher.

A charming tale of seeing through the eyes of love.

Nasreddin Hoça and the Third Shot. In Walker, *A Treasury of Turkish Folktales for Children.*

"'Listen a hundred times; ponder a thousand times; speak once,' he mourned." The Hoça brags of his archery skills to Tamerlane.

Nasreddin Hoça, Seller of Wisdom. In Walker, *A Treasury of Turkish Folktales for Children.*

"'Liras or no liras,' responded his wife, 'you must become a merchant tomorrow or I'll—I'll leave you, and take the cow right along with me.'"

The Nightingale. Wolkstein, Andersen, in Smith, *Homespun.*

"But when they heard the Nightingale sing, they all agreed, 'That is the best of all.'"

Old Dry Frye. In Chase, *Grandfather T.*

"'Law me,' he says, 'they'll find old Dry Frye here and they'll hang me for murder sure!'"

The Old Man's Wen. In Bang, *The Goblins Giggle*. Also in Uchida, *The Dancing Kettle.*

"The old man's hands started clapping to the song; his feet danced out from under him.

Kackle Kackle

Kickle Kockle."

Old One-eye. In Chase, *Grandfather Tales*. An audience participation version is in MacDonald, *Twenty Tellable Tales.*

How an old woman unknowingly scares off three robbers.

The Old Witch. Included in Jacobs, *More English Fairy Tales*. A New England version is in Tashjian, *With a Deep Sea Smile.*

"With a willy-willy wag, and a long-tailed bag,

Who's stole my money, all I had?"

The Old Woman and Her Dumpling. In Minard, *Womenfolk and Fairy Tales*. Also in Hearn, *Old Woman Who Lost Her Dumpling.*

"But the old woman only laughed and ran on farther down the road, crying, 'My dumpling, my dumpling! Where is that dumpling of mine?'"

The Old Woman and Her Pig. In Jacobs, *English Fairy Tales.*

"Stick! stick! beat dog! dog won't bite pig; piggy won't get over the stile; and I shan't get home tonight."

Oliver Hyde's Dishcloth Concert. In Kennedy, *Richard Kennedy.*

"Oliver used to have many friends. . . . But on the day his wife was buried he busted his fiddle across a porch post."

One-eye, Two-eyes, and Three-eyes. In Manheim, *Grimms' Tales for Young and Old*.

"Little goat, bleat,

Bring me a table

With good things to eat."

Oté: A Puerto Rican Folk Tale. Retold by Pura Belpre. Illustrated by Paul Galdone.

How the tiniest child in the family defeated the nearsighted devil. A colorfully illustrated picture book.

The Palace on the Rock. In Hughes, *The Wonder-Dog*.

Why the king kept his sixteen children in lobster pots.

The Pancake. In Thompson, *One Hundred Favorite Folktales*.

"One was lying in the pan, frizzling away—Ah! so beautiful and thick—it was a pleasure to look at it." A Norwegian tale.

Patrick O'Donnell and the Leprechaun. In Haviland, *Favorite Fairy Tales Told in Ireland*. Also in Pilkington, *Shamrock and Spear*, and Linda Shute, **Clever Tom and the Leprechaun**.

Patrick saves a leprechaun in return for a promise of a pot of gold.

The Peddler of Ballaghadereen, in Sawyer, *The Way of the Storyteller*. **The Dream and the Treasure**, a Jewish version, in Schram, *Jewish Stories One Generation Tells Another*. A nice picture book is Uri Shulevitz's *The Treasure*.

A kindly Peddler is told to go to town where he will hear what he needs to hear.

The Pedlar of Swaffham. In Colwell, *Round about and Long Ago*.

Perez and Martina. Pura Belpre. Illustrated by Carlos Sanchez. Also as **Martina the Beautiful Cockroach: A Cuban Folktale**, retold by Carmen Agra Deedy. Illustrated by Michael Austin. Also in Martinez, *Once Upon a Time/Habia un Vez*, which has a happy ending.

A Puerto Rican folk tale about the little cockroach, Martina, who still sings for her Perez to come back to her.

The Popcorn Blizzard. In McCormick, *Paul Bunyan Swings His Axe*.

"Even the horses thought it was real snow, and some of them almost froze to death before the men could put woolen blankets on them and lead them to shelter."

Pot of Gold. *See* **Patrick O'Donnell and the Leprechaun**.

A Pottle o' Brains. In Jacobs, *More English Fairy Tales*.

A young man must get a pottle o' brains to marry.

Prince Ivan, the Witch Baby, and the Little Sister of the Sun. In Ransome, *Old Peter's Russian Tales*.

Prince Ivan goes to the end of the world to be safe from his baby sister, who is a witch who has iron teeth and grows like a seed of corn.

The Princess on the Glass Hill. In Asbjørnsen, *East o' the Sun and West o' the Moon*.

"And there wasn't one who could get a yard or two up; and no wonder, for the hill was as smooth as a sheet of glass."

The Princess on the Pea. Andersen, in Shedlock, *Art of the Story-teller*.

"The water was running out of her hair on to her clothes, into her shoes and out at the heels; and yet she said she was a *real* Princess."

The Princess Who Always Believed What She Heard. In Hatch, *Thirteen Danish Tales*. The princess is equally skilled at telling tall tales in **Boots Who Made the Princess Say "That's a Story,"** in Asbjørnsen, *East o' the Sun and West o' the Moon*.

"It looked as if the kingdom would go to rack and ruin when the king died and there was no one to rule but a princess who could not tell right from wrong."

Pulling Teeth. In Schwartz, *Whoppers*.

"Then they all pulled as hard as they could, but they could not move the tooth."

The Pumpkin Child. In Mehdevi, *Persian Folk and Fairy Tales*.

"All the town laughed because the richest and handsomest young man in town was marrying a fat, yellow pumpkin."

Punia and the King of the Sharks. In MacDonald, *Twenty Tellable Tales*.

A brave Hawaiian boy avenges his father's death.

Pushing Up the Sky. In Clark, *Indian Legends of the Pacific Northwest*.

The creator brought many languages to the Pacific Northwest, but left the sky too low for comfort. A Snohomish tale.

Puss-in-Boots. Haviland, *Favorite Fairy Tales Told around the World*.

A young man's fortune is made by his daring cat.

The Rainbow Bird: An Aboriginal Folktale from Northern Australia. Retold by Eric Maddern. Illustrated by Adrienne Kennaway.

BirdWoman steals fire, puts it in wood, then changes to Rainbow Bird.

Rap! Rap! Rap! In Hardendorff, *Witches, Wit and a Werewolf.*
"The only sound he heard was a faint rap, rap, rap. And the sound was coming from upstairs." A shaggy dog story.

Rapunzel. In Gag, *Tales from Grimm.*
"How is it, Mother Gothel, that it takes you so long to climb up here, while the Prince can do it in just a minute—oh!"

Rattle-Rattle-Rattle and Chink-Chink-Chink. In Fillmore, *Czechoslovak Fairy Tales.*
"A man am I
Six inches high
But a long, long beard
Hangs from my chin. . . .
Open the door
And let me in!"

Raven Brings Fire. In Robinson, *Raven the Trickster.*
"'Give away fire,' he screeched, 'and have Man as mighty as Qok the Owl? Never! Go away, Raven!'"

Raven Lets Out the Daylight. In Haviland, *North American Legends.*
"Then secretly he loosened the string, and *whisk!* the silver disk of the Moon went spinning through the smoke hole."

The Red Silk Handkerchief. In MacDonald, *When the Lights Go Out.*
"A hoarse voice seemed to whisper,
'Joanne Joanne return to me
the red silk handkerchief
I gave to thee.'"

The Revenge of the Serpent. In Jewett, *Which Was Witch.*
"'Not so fast, young woodcutter!' hissed the girl. 'Neither now nor ever will you leave this hut alive.'"

The Rich Man and the Shoe-maker. By Jean de La Fontaine. Illustrated by Brian Wildsmith.
The tale of the poor but happy shoemaker who is made miserable by his new fortune.

The Ring. In Manning-Sanders, *A Book of Ghosts and Goblins.*
"My ring, I want my ring that you have stolen! I go not from here. I am on the bed now, quite, quite close to you."

The Rooster Who Would Be King. In Schram, *Jewish Stories One Generation Tells Another*. Also as **Prince Rooster**, in Jaffe, *While Standing on One Foot*.

"One day, a strange illness overcame the Prince, and he began to act like a Rooster."

Rumpelstiltskin. In Haviland, *Favorite Fairy Tales Told around the World*. Also as **Tom Tit Tot**, in Jacobs, *English Fairy Tales*. Also as **Duffy and the Devil**, a Cornish version retold by Harve Zemach. Illustrated by Margot Zemach. Also as **Whuppety Stoorie**. John Warren Stewig. Illustrated by Preston McDaniels. Also in **Whuppety Stoorie**. Carolyn White. Illustrated by S. D. Schindler. Scotch-Irish variants.

"But he answered only, 'No, that is not my name.'"

Salt. In Ransome, *Old Peter's Russian Tales*. Also in Afanasev, *Russian Fairy Tales*. "That is the story about salt, and how it made a rich man of Ivan the Ninny, and besides gave him the prettiest wife in the world, and she a Tsar's daughter."

The Scary Song. In Winn, *The Fireside Book of Fun and Game Songs*. A traditional song from the Southern Appalachian mountains. Also known as **There Was an Old Lady All Skin and Bones.** A good "jump" story-song for Halloween.

The Sea of Gold. In Uchida, *The Sea of Gold*. "For under the light of the moon, the sand glittered and sparkled like a beach of gold." A simple and generous ship's cook is rewarded by the King of the Sea.

The Selfish Giant. In Wilde, *The Happy Prince*. "And the Giant's heart melted as he looked out. 'How selfish I have been!' he said; 'now I know why the Spring would not come here.'"

The Selkie Girl. Retold by Susan Cooper. Illustrated by Warwick Hutton. The ancient tale of a seal-girl and a fisherman who catches her.

Seven at One Blow. *See* **Brave in Spite of Himself.**

Seven Sleepers of Ephesus. In Spaulding, *The Wisdom of Storytelling in an Information Age*. An old legend from Christian and Muslim traditions.

The Shepherd's Nosegay. In Fillmore, *The Shepherd's Nosegay*. Also in Haviland, *Favorite Fairy Tales from Czechoslovakia*.

"The Princess was a merry girl, so she laughed and said: 'Yanitchko, please give me that nosegay.'"

The Shepherd's Pipe. In Mincieli, *Tales Merry and Wise*.

"But the good mother looked at him and said softly, 'Come closer to the manger for the Bambino cannot hear your music if you play it so far away.'"

The Shoemaker and the Elves. In Gag, *More Tales from Grimm*.

"In the morning, there again were the shoes—two pairs this time—all ready to wear."

Shrewd Todie and Lyzer the Miser. In Singer, *When Shlemiel Went to Warsaw*.

"And Todie said, 'Your tablespoon gave birth to a teaspoon. It is her child." Also a Hodja story.

The Silly Jelly Fish. In Hearn, *Japanese Fairy Tales*.

Why the jellyfish is boneless.

The Singing Tortoise. In Courlander, *The Cow-tail Switch and Other West African Stories*. Another story of a man who couldn't keep a secret is **Musakalala, the Talking Skull**, in Littledale, *Ghosts and Spirits*.

"I'll bring the tortoise here. She will sing and play for you. If she can't do this, then you may beat me for it!"

Sir Gawain and the Loathly Lady. Retold by Selina Hastings. Illustrated by Juan Wijngaard.

"I shall give you one chance to save both your kingdom and your life. . . . What is it that women most desire?"

The Skeleton Man. In Gustafson, *Monster Rolling Skull*. Another version of this Native American horror story is **The Vampire Skeleton**, in Bruchac, *Iroquois Stories*.

"But her husband was gone . . . *and the skeleton's hand no longer hung over the side of the box!*"

The Skull. In Manning-Sanders, *A Book of Ghosts and Goblins*.

"At midnight the skeleton will come and try to snatch me away from you. But hold me tight, hold me tight!"

The Sky God's Daughter. In Courlander, *The King's Drum and Other African Stories*.

"The first man who discovers my daughter's secret name, he shall be my son-in-law."

The Sleeping Beauty. In Rackham, *The Arthur Rackham Fairy Book.*
"The very spits before the kitchen-fire ceased turning, the fire went out, and everything became as silent as in the dead of night."

Smoking. In Spaulding, *The Wisdom of Storytelling in an Information Age.*
A parable on the importance of choosing language carefully. A Zen story.

Snowflake. In Carrick, *Picture Tales from the Russian.* For older children, try **Snegourka**, in Shedlock, *Art of the Story-teller.*
"Look here, my dear, let's go and make a little girl out of snow; we'll call her Snowflake, and she'll be like a little daughter to us."

Soap, Soap, Soap! In Chase, *Grandfather Tales.* Also in the picture book, **Soap! Soap! Don't Forget the Soap!** Retold by Tom Birdseye. Illustrated by Andrew Glass. Another funny story about a boy's calamitous trip to the store is **Just Say Hiç!** [salt] in Walker, *A Treasury of Turkish Folktales for Children.* A retelling that lends itself to audience participation is **Hiç! Hiç! Hiç!** in MacDonald, *Twenty Tellable Tales.*
"Right there I had it—
Right there I lost it."

Sody Sallyraytus. In Chase, *Grandfather Tales.*
"When she got to the bridge the old bear stuck his head out—'*I* EAT A LITTLE BOY, HIM AND HIS SODY SALLYRAYTUS—AND I'LL EAT YOU TOO!'"

Soldier Jack. In Chase, *The Jack Tales.* Another amusing version, **The Magic Pepino Vine**, in de Osma, *Witches' Ride and Other Tales from Costa Rica.*
"'Why, ain't you heard?' the old lady asked him. 'Some fool's got death shut up in a sack. There ain't nobody died around here for a hundred and forty-two years'"

Sop Doll! In Chase, *The Jack Tales.*
"Then that cat fopped its foot smack in Jack's gravy, says, 'Sop! Doll-ll-ll!'"

The Sorcerer's Apprentice. In Gag, *More Tales from Grimm.*
"Now the boy knew that he was not working for an ordinary magician, but for a cruel, dangerous sorcerer."

The Soup Stone. *See* **Stone Soup**.

Spindle, Shuttle, and Needle. Grimm, in Segal, *The Juniper Tree and Other Tales from Grimm*. Also in Gag, *Tales from Grimm*.

"Spindle, spindle, one two three,
Bring my suitor home to me."

The Squire's Bride. In Asbjørnsen, *Norwegian Folk Tales*.

"She wouldn't have the Squire if he sat in powdered gold up to his ears, she said."

The Steadfast Tin Soldier. In Andersen, *It's Perfectly True and Other Stories*. Also in Andersen, *Eighty Fairy Tales*.

"He looked at the little lady, she looked at him, and he felt that he was melting, but he stood steadfast with shouldered arms."

Stone Soup. Retold and illustrated by Marcia Brown. Also in Maria Leach. *The Soup Stone*. **Nail Soup**, a Swedish version, is in Yolen, *Favorite Folktales from around the World*.

"'A good stone soup should have a cabbage,' said the soldiers, as they sliced the carrots into the pot. 'But no use asking for what you don't have.'"

The Storyteller. In Courlander, *The Fire on the Mountain and Other Ethiopian Stories*.

"'But there are so many ants in the story'; the farmer said, 'And the next day another ant came for a grain of wheat.'"

The Strange Visitor. In Jacobs, *English Fairy Tales*. A very short American variant is **What Do You Come For?** in Schwartz, *Scary Stories*.

"In came a pair of huge huge hands, and sat down
on the small small arms;
And still she sat, and still she reeled,
and still she wished for company."

The Straw, the Coal and the Bean. In Manheim, *Grimm's Tales for Young and Old*.

A silly pourquoi about the sad fate of these three friends.

Strega Nona. *See* **The Magic Porridge Pot**.

The Swineherd. Andersen, in Shedlock, *Art of the Story-teller*.

"'Fie, papa!' she said, 'it is not made at all: it is a natural rose!'"

The Tailor. In Schimmel, *Just Enough to Make a Story*.

A poor but industrious tailor turns a coat into a jacket, and, at last, a button into a story.

The Tailypo. *See* **Chunk o' Meat**.

'Tain't so. In Leach, *Whistle in the Graveyard*.

"The whole town knew that old man Dinkins was dead; but old man Dinkins sat on the graveyard fence saying, ''Tain't so.'"

The Tale of a Black Cat. In MacDonald, *When the Lights Go Out*. This classic drawing story is also in Pellowski, *Story Vine*.

"Climbed out of that puddle . . . just went two steps . . . and they fell down in a *mud puddle* again."

Talk. In Courlander, *The Cow-tail Switch and Other West African Stories*. A U.S. version is **The Talking Mule**. In Durell, *The Diane Goode Book of American Folk Tales and Songs*.

"'Fantastic, isn't it?' his stool said. 'Imagine, a talking yam!'"

The Talking Pot. In Hatch, *Thirteen Danish Tales*. Also as **The Wonderful Pot**, in Haviland, *Favorite Fairy Tales Told around the World*.

"'Take me, take me,' cried the pot, 'and you'll never have cause to rue it.'"

Tamlane. In Jacobs, *More English Fairy Tales*. Also in **Tam Lin**. Retold by Susan Cooper. Illustrated by Warwick Hutton.

"Then seize me quick, and whatever change befall me . . . cling hold to me till they turn me into red-hot iron."

Tattercoats. In Jacobs, *More English Fairy Tales*.

"But the more she refused him the sweeter the pipe played, and the deeper the young man fell in love."

Teeny-Tiny. In Jacobs, *English Fairy Tales*.

"So the teeny-tiny woman put the teeny-tiny bone into her teeny-tiny pocket, and went home to her teeny-tiny house."

Teeny-Tiny and the Witch-Woman. In Walker, *Treasury of Turkish Folktales for Children*.

"'Who is asleep and who is awake?' called the old woman. And, 'The littlest one is awake: answered Teeny-Tiny.'"

The Tengu's Magic Nose Fan. In Uchida, *Sea of Gold and Other Tales from Japan*.

"Fan it with one side and your nose will grow. Fan it with the other side and your nose will shrink. It's that kind of nose fan."

The Terrible Leak. In Uchida, *The Magic Listening Cap*.

"Well, the one thing I fear most of all right now is a leak! And I'm afraid one may come along any minute!"

The Terrible Olli. In Fillmore, *The Shepherd's Nosegay*. Also in Fenner, *Giants and Witches and a Dragon or Two*.

"Well after that no other troll ever dared settle on that side of the mountain. They were all too afraid of the Terrible Olli!"

Then Your Wisdom Is Wasted. In Spaulding, *The Wisdom of Storytelling in an Information Age*.

A parable from India about the value of book learning versus that of life.

The Thing at the Foot of the Bed. In Leach, *The Thing at the Foot of the Bed and Other Scary Tales*.

"Once there was a man and they dared him to sleep all night in a haunted House."

The Three Bears. In Bryant, *How to Tell Stories to Children*. Another version is **Goldilocks and the Three Bears**, in Crossley-Holland, *British Fairy Tales*.

"'SOMEBODY HAS BEEN LYING IN MY BED,—AND HERE SHE IS!' said the Little Small Wee Bear, in his little, small, wee voice."

The Three Billy-Goats Gruff. In Asbjørnsen, *East o' the Sun and West o' the Moon*. Also in Haviland, *The Fairy Tale Treasury*. Also in the picture book, **The Three Billy Goats Gruff**. Illustrated by Marcia Brown.

"Well, come along! I've got two spears,
and I'll poke your eyeballs out at your ears."

Three Fridays. In Kelsey, *Once the Hodja*. Also in Sutherland, *The Scott Foresman Anthology of Children's Literature*.

A funny story about how the hodja cleverly solved his weekly problem of preaching a sermon.

The Three Little Pigs. In Jacobs, *English Fairy Tales*.

"Then I'll huff, and I'll puff, and I'll blow your house in."

The Three Sillies. In Jacobs, *English Fairy Tales*. Also shortened as **Clever Elsie**, in Gag, *Tales from Grimm*.

"When I can find three bigger sillies than you three, then I'll come back and marry your daughter."

The Three Spinners. In Gag, *More Tales from Grimm*.

"The first had a broad flat foot; the second had an enormous, drooping underlip . . . and the third had such a big clumsy thumb that it was beyond all belief."

Three Strong Women (A Tall Tale from Japan). Stamm, in Minard, *Womenfolk and Fairy Tales*.

"How Forever Mountain, a strong and confident sumo wrestler, met his match in a cheerful, round young girl."

The Three Wishes. In Jacobs, *More English Fairy Tales*. Also in Zemach, *The Three Wishes*.

"And before you could say Jack Robinson, there the goodman sat and his nose as the longer for a noble link of black pudding."

Ticky-picky Boom-boom. In Sherlock, *Anansi, the Spider Man*.

"Down the road came the yams, stamping on their two legs, three legs, four legs:
'Ticky-Picky Boom-Boom,
Ticky-Picky Boom-Boom, Boof!'"

The Tiger and the Rabbit. In Belpre, *The Tiger & Rabbit*.

"'Aha!' he cried. 'Today, I will eat you up.' 'Of course you will.' answered the Rabbit, 'but first, do have a taste of this delicious cheese.'"

The Tiger, the Brahman and the Jackal. In Jacobs, *Indian Folk & Fairy Tales*.

"Let me see—the tiger was in the Brahman, and the cage came walking by—no, that's not it, either!"

The Tiger's Whisker. In Courlander, *The Tiger's Whisker and Other Tales and Legends from Asia and the Pacific*. Also in Cole, *Best-loved Folk Tales of the World*.

To heal her husband, home from war, a woman tames a tiger.

Tikki Tikki Tembo. Retold by Arlene Mosel. Illustrated by Blair Lent. A version in which Tikki does not survive is in Hardendorff, *The Frog's Saddle Horse*.

"Oh, Most Honorable Mother, Tikki tikki tembo-no- sa- rembo-chari bari ruchi-pip peri pembo has fallen into the well!"

The Tinder-box. In Andersen, *It's Perfectly True and Other Stories*. Also Keigwin, in Andersen, *Eighty Fairy Tales*.

"One, two, three! Look! There were all the dogs, the one with eyes as big as saucers, the one with eyes like mill-wheels, and the one with eyes as big as the Round Tower."

The Tinker and the Ghost. Boggs and Davis, in Yolen, *Favorite Folktales from around the World*. Also in Manning-Sanders, *A Book of Ghosts and Goblins*, as **A Box on the Ear**.

"On the wide plain not far from the city of Toledo there once stood a great gray castle. For many years before this story begins no one had dwelt there, because the castle was haunted."

To Your Good Health. In Shedlock, *Art of the Story-teller*.

Whenever the King sneezed, "everyone in the whole country had to say, 'To your good health!' Everyone said it except the Shepherd with the bright blue eyes, and he would not say it."

Toads and Diamonds. In Rackham, *The Arthur Rackham Fairy Book*.

"'What can this be?' said her mother, in amazement. 'I really do believe that pearls and diamonds are falling from the girl's mouth!'"

A retelling from Perrault.

Tom-Tit-Tot. *See* **Rumplestiltskin**.

The Tongue-cut Sparrow. In Uchida, *The Dancing Kettle, and Other Japanese Folk Tales*.

"Tongue-cut sparrow, where are you now?

Tongue-cut sparrow, where is your home?"

The Town Mouse and the Country Mouse. In Jacobs, *The Fables of Aesop*.

"Better beans and bacon in peace than cakes and ale in fear."

The Treasure. In Hatch, *More Danish Tales*.

When a poor peasant finds a buried treasure his wife is eager to tell the neighbors.

The Trial of the Stone. In Courlander, *The Tiger's Whisker and Other Tales and Legends from Asia and the Pacific*.

"The townspeople looked at one another and tried not to laugh . . . while the chief asked the stone questions." Burmese tale of justice.

Truth Learns about Welcome. In Spaulding, *The Wisdom of Story-telling in an Information Age*.

A brief parable about how people find it hard to listen to truth. A Yiddish version is found in Ausubel, *Treasury of Jewish Folklore*.

Tug-of-War. In Lester, *How Many Spots Does a Leopard Have?* Bo Rabbit tricks Whale and Elephant in the title story of Priscilla Jaquith's collection *Bo Rabbit*.

"Have you ever noticed how the littlest things have the most mouth?"

The Turnip. Tolstoy, in Haviland, *The Fairy Tale Treasury*. Can be a participation story.

"Grow, grow, little turnip, grow sweet!

Grow, grow, little turnip, grow strong!"

The Twelve Dancing Princesses. In Lang (or Alderson), *Red Fairy Book*. Also in de la Mare, *Tales, Told Again*.

Soldier tracks where princesses go at night to dance. De la Mare's version is witty and better than Lang's for telling.

Twelve Great Black Cats and the Red One. In Leodhas, *Twelve Great Black Cats*. Also In MacDonald, *When the Lights Go Out*, as **The Great Red Cat** (shorter).

How Murdo Mac Taggart was saved on a wild stormy all Hallowmass Eve from the devil himself and a pack of his demons from hell.

The Twelve Months. In Haviland, *Favorite Fairy Tales Told around the World..*

"'Apples in winter!' exclaimed Marushka. 'Why, the trees have neither leaves nor fruit on them now.'" Also known as **The Month Brothers**.

The Twist-mouth Family. In Durell, *The Diane Goode Book of American Folk Tales and Songs*. Also in Tashjian, *Juba This and Juba That*, as **The Snooks Family**.

A silly story that depends on gesture for its effect.

Two of Everything. In Ritchie, *The Treasure of Li-Po*. Also in Sutherland, *The Scott Foresman Anthology of Children's Literture*. Also in *Two of Everything*. Retold by Lily Toy Hong.

A magic pot produces two of everything, including Mrs. Hak-Tak.

The Two Old Women's Bet. In Chase, *Grandfather Tales*.

"One time there were two old women got to talkin' about the men folks . . . so fin'lly they made a bet which one could make the biggest fool of her husband."

Unanana and the Elephant. In Minard, *Womenfolk and Fairy Tales*.

"I don't know why it is, but ever since I swallowed that woman called Unanana, I have felt most uncomfortable and unsettled inside."

Under the Cherry Blossom Tree. Retold by Allen Say.

An outrageously silly story about a greedy landlord.

The Unlucky Shoes of Ali Abou. In Carpenter, *The Elephant's Bathtub*.

"Yes, put these shoes in jail. Never let them come near me again." A humorous story about a miser's problems.

Urashima. In Cole, *Best-loved Folk Tales of the World*.

Urashima travels with the Dragon Princess to her marvelous home under the sea. A Japanese Rip Van Winkle story.

The Valiant Chattee-maker. In Baker, *The Talking Tree*. Also In Haviland, *Favorite Fairy Tales Told around the World*. Similar to **The Terrible Leak**.

"The chattee-maker, having made the tiger get up, got on its back and forced it to carry him home . . . for all this time he fancied he was on his donkey."

Vasilisa the Beautiful. Afanas'ev, in Yolen, *Favorite Folktales from around the World*.

"The doll answered, 'Fear not, Vasilisa the Beautiful! Eat your supper, say your prayers, and go to sleep; the morning is wiser than the evening.'"

The Wave. Adapted by Margaret Hodges. Illustrated by Blair Lent. From Hearn, **Gleanings in Buddha-Fields**.

How Ojiisan set fire to his rice fields to save the people of his village from disaster.

The Wedding of the Mouse. In Uchida, *The Dancing Kettle*.

"Why, she is so fair and so lovely, only the greatest being in this whole wide world would be worthy of her."

The Wedding Procession of the Rag Doll and the Broom Handle and Who Was in It. In Sandburg, *Rootabaga Stories*.

"Well, first came the Spoon Lickers."

The Well of the World's End. In Jacobs, *English Fairy Tales*.

"Open the door, my hinny, my heart,

Open the door, my own darling;

Mind you the words that you and I spoke

Down in the meadow, at the World's End."

When Shlemiel Went to Warsaw. In Singer, *When Shlemiel Went to Warsaw*. Another absentminded traveler is **The Scholar of Kosei**, in Courlander, *The Tiger's Whisker and Other Tales and Legends from Asia and the Pacific*.

"Shlemiel paused a moment and then he said: 'Mrs. Shlemiel, I'm not your husband. Children, I'm not your papa.'"

Which Was Witch? In Jewett, *Which Was Witch?* Also in Sutherland, *The Scott Foresman Anthology of Children's Literature*.

They were identical as twins. One was a witch and one was his wife, but which was which? From Korea.

The White Horse Girl and the Blue Wind Boy. In Sandburg, *Rootabaga Stories*.

"To All Our Sweethearts, Old Folks and Young Folks: We have started to go where the white horses come from and where the blue winds begin. Keep a corner in your hearts for us while we are gone."

Who Can Break a Bad Habit? In Carpenter, *African Wonder Tales*. Also in MacDonald, *Twenty Tellable Tales*, as **How to Break a Bad Habit**.

An amusing story of a contest between a rabbit and a monkey in which gesture plays an important part.

Who's in Rabbit's House? Retold by Verna Aardema. Illustrated by Leo and Diane Dillon.

"The bad voice replied, 'I am the Long One. I eat trees and trample on elephants. Go away! or I will trample on you!'"

Why Mosquitoes Buzz in People's Ears. Retold by Verna Aardema. Illustrated by Leo and Diane Dillon.

"Did you hear?
It was the monkey
Who killed the owlet and
now Mother Owl won't wake the sun
so that the day can come."

Why the Bear Is Stumpy-tailed. In Asbjørnsen, *East o' the Sun and West o' the Moon*.

"You're not to mind if your tail smarts a little; that's when the fish bite."

Why the Sea Is Salt. *See* **The Mill That Grinds at the Bottom of the Sea**.

Why the Sky Is Far Away. In Spaulding, *The Wisdom of Storytelling in an Information Age*. Also as Mary-Joan Gerson. *Why the Sky Is Far Away: A Folktale from Nigeria*. Illustrated by Hope Meryman. Also, *Why the Sky Is Far Away: A Nigerian Folktale*. Illustrated by Carla Golembe.

An African tale. Human greed is the reason that we no longer can reach the sky and eat it.

Why the Years Are Named for Animals. In Pellowski, *The Stone Vine*.
A short tale for Chinese New Year.

Wicked John and the Devil. In Chase, *Grandfather Tales*. Also in
MacDonald, *When the Lights Go Out*.
"Well, John, I'm Saint Peter . . . and the first man treats me right I
always give him three wishes."

Wiley and the Hairy Man. By Molly Garrett Bang.
"Wiley's mother said, 'Wiley be careful when you go to the swamp.
. . . The Hairy Man will get you if you don't watch out.'" A longer
version is in Hamilton, *People Fly*.

Wind and Sun. Included in Reeves, *Fables from Aesop*.
"Wind and Sun had an argument one day, about which was the
stronger."

Wings. Sologub, in Tyler, *Twenty-four Unusual Stories*.
"The princess laughed scornfully and exclaimed, 'What a foolish
girl! . . . No one who is not a princess can ever grow wings.'" Diane
Wolkstein retells it as *The Magic Wings*.

The Winning of Kwelanga. In Aardema, *Behind the Back of the
Mountain*.
The beautiful princess sings magic songs to help her handsome
suitor succeed in the tasks her father has set.

The Winter of the Blue Snow. In McCormick, *Paul Bunyan Swings
His Axe*.
"It was so cold that when Hot Biscuit Slim set the coffee out to cool
it froze so fast the ice was hot."

Winter Rose. In Lin, *The Milky Way and Other Chinese Folk Tales*.
Two brave sisters outwit an evil wizard and escape in his invisible
gown to bring rose petals for their sick mother.

The Wise Old Woman. In Uchida, *The Sea of Gold*. Also in Yoshiko
Uchida's picture book version, *The Wise Old Woman*. Illustrated by
Martin Springett.
"'I have no use for old people in my village,' he said haughtily. 'I
therefore decree that anyone over seventy-one must be banished
from the village.'"

Wishes. In Babbitt, *The Devil's Storybook*.
The Devil dresses as a fairy godmother to tempt three people.

Witches of Ashkelon. In Schwartz, *Elijah's Violin*.

Rabbi Shimon must think of a plan to rid his city of the eighty evil witches who plague it.

The Witches' Ride. In de Osma, *The Witches' Ride*. Also in Clarkson, *World Folktales*.

What happened when the bobo rode on a witch's broom.

The Witch's Skin (La Bruja del Cuero). In Alegria, *The Three Wishes*.

"Every night . . . his wife, who was a witch, went out to a guava tree . . . and there she took off the skin that covered her witch's body and hung it on the tree." A story from Puerto Rico.

With a Wig, with a Wag. *See* **The Old Witch**.

The Wolf and the Seven Little Kids. Crane, in Grimm, *Household Stories from the Collection of the Brothers Grimm*. Also in *The Wolf and the Seven Little Kids*. Illustrated by Felix Hoffman.

"'First show us your paws,' said the kids, 'so that we may know if you are really our mother or not.'"

The Woman and the Tree Children. In Lester, *How Many Spots Does a Leopard Have?*

"You are nothing but a child of the tree. . . . One can't expect any better from children born out of a tree." A story from Africa.

The Woman Who Flummoxed the Fairies. In Leodhas-Alger, *Heather and Broom*. Also in Minard, *Womenfolk and Fairy Tales*.

"Not only was she a master baker, but she was the cleverest woman in the world; and it was the first that got her into trouble, but it was the second that got her out of it."

The Women Who Ate Onions. In Monroe, *They Dance in the Sky*.

A funny myth from California. Women discover wild onions and ruin their husbands' hunting.

The Wonderful Pot. *See* **The Talking Pot**.

The Woodcutter of Gura. In Courlander, *The Fire on the Mountain and Other Ethiopian Stories*. Also in Courlander, *The Piece of Fire and Other Haitian Tales*, as **Bouki Cuts Wood**.

"So, thinking he was dead, the woodcutter didn't try to get up at all, but just lay there without moving."

Yeh-Shen: A Cinderella Story from China. Retold by Ai-Ling Louie. Illustrated by Ed Young.

"'Be sure you do not lose your golden shoes,' said the spirit of the bones."

The Yellow Ribbon. Leach, in Tashjian, *Juba This and Juba That*.

"One day John said, 'Jane, why do you wear that yellow ribbon around your neck?'"

Zlateh the Goat. In Singer, *Zlateh the Goat*.

Aaron and his pet goat are caught in a snowstorm during Hanukkah. A story of love and survival.

Story Collections

The audience itself was a performance. Moving, shifting, laughing, clapping, all as one, as if they were all part of the same soul.

—Orson Scott Card[1]

Some older titles are available online. Refer to appendix C for sources if you don't have access to a good library.

Aardema, Verna. *Behind the Back of the Mountain: Black Folktales from Southern Africa*. Dial, 1973.

Ada, Alma Flor, and F. Isabel Campoy. *Tales Our Abuelitas Told: A Hispanic Folklore Collection*. Atheneum, 2006.

Aesop. *The Fables of Aesop*. Selected, told anew, and their history traced by Joseph Jacobs. Schocken, 1966.

———. *The McElderry Book of Aesop's Fables*. Adapted by Michael Morpurgo. McElderry, 2005.

———. www.aesopfables.com/aesopjdlf.html (accessed June 15, 2010).

Afanasyev, Alexander. *Russian Fairy Tales*. Translated by Norbert Guterman. Pantheon, 1975.

Alegria, Ricardo E. *The Three Wishes: A Collection of Puerto Rican Folktales*. Harcourt, Brace & World, 1969.

American Storytelling Series. Wilson Video Resource Collection. 1986. Video series.

Andersen, Hans Christian. *Eighty Fairy Tales*. Translated by R. P. Keigwin. Pantheon, 1976.

———. *It's Perfectly True and Other Stories*. Translated by Paul Leyssac. Harcourt, Brace & World, 1966.

Asbjørnsen, Peter Christen, and Jørgen Moe. *East o' the Sun and West o' the Moon: Fifty-nine Norwegian Folk Tales from the Collection of Peter Christen Asbjørnsen and Jørgen Moe.* Translated by George Webbe Dasent. Dover, 1970.

——. *Norwegian Folk Tales from the Collection of Peter Christen Asbjørnsen and Jørgen Moe.* Translated by Pat Shaw and Carl Norman. Pantheon, 1960.

Association for Childhood Education International. *Told under the Green Umbrella.* Macmillan, 1958.

——. *Told Under the Magic Umbrella.* Macmillan, 1930.

Ausubel, Nathan. *A Treasury of Jewish Folklore.* Crown, 1989.

Babbitt, Natalie. *The Devil's Storybook.* Farrar, Straus & Giroux, 1974.

Badoe, Adwoa. *The Pot of Wisdom: Ananse Stories.* Douglas & McIntyre, 2001.

Baker, Augusta. *The Golden Lynx.* Lippincott, 1960.

——. *The Talking Tree.* Lippincott, 1955.

Baltuck, Naomi. *Apples from Heaven: Multicultural Folktales about Stories and Storytellers.* Linnet, 1995.

Bang, Molly. *The Goblins Giggle and Other Stories.* Selected and illustrated by Molly Bang. Peter Smith, 1988.

Barton, Bob. *Tell Me Another.* Pembroke, 1986.

Bauer, Caroline Feller. *Celebrations: Read-Aloud Holiday and Theme Book Programs.* Wilson, 1985.

——. *New Handbook for Storytellers with Stories, Poems, Magic and More.* Revised ed. ALA, 1993.

Beier, Ulli, ed. *The Origin of Life and Death: African Creation Myths.* Heinemann, 1966.

Belpre, Pura. *The Tiger and the Rabbit and Other Tales.* Eliseo Torres, 1977.

Bennett, William. *The Book of Virtues: A Treasury of Great Moral Stories.* Simon & Schuster, 1993.

Bialik, Hayim Nahman, and Yehoshua Hana Ravnitzky, eds. *The Book of Legends Sefer Ha-Aggadah: Legends from the Talmud and Midrash.* Translated by William G. Braude. Schocken, 1992.

Bierhorst, John. *The Girl Who Married a Ghost.* Four Winds, 1978.

Briggs, Katherine. *British Folk Tales.* Dorset, 1989.

Brinkerhoff, Shirley. *Contemporary Folklore.* Mason Crest, 2003.

Bruchac, Joseph. *Iroquois Stories: Heroes and Heroines; Monsters and Magic.* Crossing Press, 1985.

Brunvand, Jan Harold, ed. *The Big Book of Urban Legends.* Paradox Press, 1994.

——. *Encyclopedia of Urban Legends.* ABC-CLIO, 2001.

Bryan, Ashley. *Ashley Bryan's African Tales, Uh-Huh*. Atheneum, 1998.

Bryant, Sara Cone. *How to Tell Stories to Children*. Omnigraphics, 1990.

Burns, Batt. *The King with Horse's Ears and Other Irish Fairy Tales*. Sterling, 2009.

Calvino, Italo. *Italian Folktales*. Harvest, 1992.

Carpenter, Frances. *African Wonder Tales*. Doubleday, 1963.

———. *The Elephant's Bathtub*. Doubleday, 1962.

Carrick, Valery. *Picture Folk-tales*. Dover, 1992.

———. *Picture Tales from the Russian*. Dufour, 1966.

Carter, Dorothy Sharp. *Greedy Mariani and Other Folktales of the Antilles*. Atheneum, 1974.

Chase, Richard. *Grandfather Tales*. Houghton Mifflin, 2003.

———. *The Jack Tales*. Houghton Mifflin, 2003.

Chrisman, Arthur Bowie. *Shen of the Sea*. Dutton, 1968.

Clark, Ella E. *Indian Legends of the Pacific Northwest*. University of California Press, 1953.

Clarkson, Atelia, and Gilbert B. Cross. *World Folktales: A Scribner Resource Collection*. Scribners, 1984.

Cole, Joanna. *Best-loved Folk Tales of the World*. Anchor, 1983.

Colwell, Eileen. *Round About and Long Ago: Tales from the English Counties*. Houghton Mifflin, 1974.

Courlander, Harold. *Kantchil's Lime Pit and Other Stories from Indonesia*. Harcourt, Brace & World, 1950.

———. *The King's Drum and Other African Stories*. Harcourt, Brace & World, 1962.

———. *The Piece of Fire and Other Haitian Tales*. Harcourt, Brace & World, 1942.

———. *The Tiger's Whisker and Other Tales and Legends from Asia and the Pacific*. Harcourt, Brace & World, 1959.

———. *Treasury of African Folklore*. Marlowe, 1996.

Courlander, Harold, with Albert Kofe Prempeh. *The Hat-shaking Dance and Other Ashanti Tales from Ghana*. Harcourt Brace Jovanovich, 1957.

Courlander, Harold, and George Herzog. *The Cow-tail Switch and Other West African Stories*. Holt, 1995.

Courlander, Harold, and Wolf Leslau. *The Fire on the Mountain and Other Ethiopian Stories*. Holt, Rinehart & Winston, 1995.

Credle, Ellis. *Tall Tales from the High Hills*. T. Nelson, 1957.

Creedon, Sharon. *Fair Is Fair: World Folktales of Justice*. August House, 1994.

Crossley-Holland, Kevin. *British Folk Tales: New Versions*. Orchard, 1987.

Daly, Ita. *Irish Myths and Legends*. Oxford University Press, 2001.

De Almeida, Livia Maria Melibeu, and Ana Maria Carnieiro Portella. *Brazilian Folktales*. Edited by Margaret Read MacDonald. Libraries Unlimited, 2006.

de la Mare, Walter. *Tales, Told Again*. Faber & Faber, 1980.

de Osma, Lupe. *Witches' Ride and Other Tales from Costa Rica*. Morrow, 1957.

deVos, Gail. *Storytelling for Young Adults: A Guide to Tales for Teens*. Libraries Unlimited, 2003.

Durell, Ann. *The Diane Goode Book of American Folk Tales and Songs*. Dutton, 1989.

Eaton, Anne Thaxter. *The Animals' Christmas*. Viking, 1972.

Erdoes, Richard. *The Sound of Flutes*. Pantheon, 1976.

Fang, Linda. *The Ch'i-lin Purse: A Collection of Ancient Chinese Stories*. Farrar, Straus & Giroux, 1995.

Farjeon, Eleanor. *Martin Pippin in the Daisy Field*. Lippincott, 1937.

Fenner, Phillis. *Ghosts, Ghosts, Ghosts*. Watts, 1952.

———. *Giants and Witches and a Dragon or Two*. Knopf, 1943.

Fillmore, Parker. *Czechoslovak Fairy Tales*. AMS Press, 1980.

———. *The Shepherd's Nosegay*. Edited by Katherine Love. Harcourt, Brace, 1958.

Finger, Charles J. *Tales from Silver Lands*. Doubleday, 1989.

Forest, Heather. *Wisdom Tales from around the World: Fifty Gems of Story and Wisdom from Such Diverse Traditions as Sufi, Zen, Taoist, Christian, Jewish, Buddhist, African and Native American*. August House, 1997.

———. *Wonder Tales from around the World*. August House, 1996.

Gag, Wanda. *More Tales from Grimm*. University of Minnesota Press, 2006.

———. *Tales from Grimm*. Coward-McCann, 1981.

Garcia, Emmett Shkeme. *Coyote and the Sky: How the Sun, Moon, and Stars Began*. University of New Mexico Press, 2006.

Gonzalez, Lucia M. *Señor Cat's Romance and Other Favorite Stories from Latin America*. Scholastic, 1997.

Greene, Ellin. *Clever Cooks*. Lothrop, Lee & Shepard, 1973.

Grimm, Jacob. *Household Stories from the Collection of the Brothers Grimm*. Translated by Lucy Crane. Dover, 1963.

Guard, Jean, and Ray A. Williamson. *They Dance in the Sky: Native American Star*. Houghton Mifflin, 2007.

Gustafson, Anita. *Monster Rolling Skull and Other Native American Tales*. Crowell, 1980.

Hamilton, Virginia. *The Dark Way: Stories from the Spirit World*. Harcourt Brace Jovanovich, 1990.

——. *Her Stories: African American Folktales, Fairy Tales, and True Tales*. Scholastic, 1995.

——. *In the Beginning: Creation Stories from around the World*. Harcourt Brace Jovanovich, 1988.

——. *The People Could Fly*. Knopf, 1985.

Hardendorff, Jeanne B. *The Frog's Saddle Horse and Other Tales*. Lippincott, 1968.

——. *Witches, Wit and a Werewolf*. Lippincott, 1971.

Harper, Wilhelmina. *Merry Christmas to You*. Dutton, 1935.

Hatch, Mary C. *More Danish Tales*. Harcourt, Brace & World, 1949.

——. *Thirteen Danish Tales*. Harcourt, Brace & World, 1947.

Haviland, Virginia. *The Fairy Tale Treasury*. Coward-McCann & Geoghegan, 1966.

——. *Favorite Fairy Tales Told around the World*. Little, Brown, 1985.

——. *Favorite Fairy Tales Told in Denmark*. Little, Brown, 1971.

——. *Favorite Fairy Tales Told in Ireland*. Little, Brown, 1961.

——. *Favorite Fairy Tales Told in Spain*. Little, Brown, 1963.

——. *North American Legends*. Collins, 1979.

Hawthorne, Nathaniel. *Tanglewood Tales for Boys and Girls*. Houghton Mifflin, 1853.

——. *Wonderbook for Girls and Boys*. Houghton Mifflin, 1852.

Hearn, Lafcadio. *Gleanings in Buddha-fields*. Cosimo Classics, 2004.

——. *Japanese Fairy Tales*. Liveright, 1953.

Heins, Ethel. *The Cat and the Cook: And Other Fables of Krylov*. Greenwillow, 1995.

Holt, David, and Bill Mooney. *More Ready-to-Tell Tales from around the World*. August House, 2000.

——. *Ready-to-tell Tales*. August House, 1994.

Hughes, Richard. *The Wonder-dog, the Collected Children's Stories of Richard Hughes*. Greenwillow, 1977.

Hume, Lotta Carswell. *Favorite Children's Stories from China and Tibet*. Tuttle, 1989.

Hurston, Zora Neale. *Lies & Other Tall Tales*. HarperCollins, 2005.

Jablow, Alta, and Carl Withers. *Man in the Moon*. Holt, Rinehart and Winston, 1969.

Jacobs, Joseph. *Celtic Fairy Tales*. Dover, 1968.

——. *English Fairy Tales*. Dover, 1967.

——. *More English Fairy Tales*. Amereon, 1894.

Jaffe, Nina, and Steve Zeitlin. *While Standing on One Foot: Puzzle Stories and Wisdom Tales from the Jewish Tradition.* Illustated by John Segal. Holt, 1993.

Jaquith, Priscilla. *Bo Rabbit Smart for True.* Philomel, 1981.

Jewett, Eleanore M. *Which Was Witch?* Viking, 1953.

Johnson, Edna, Evelyn R. Sickels, Frances Clarke Sayers, and Carolyn Horovitz. *Anthology of Children's Literature.* 5th ed. Houghton Mifflin, 1977.

Keding, Dan. *Stories of Hope and Spirit: Folktales from Eastern Europe.* August House, 2004.

Kelsey, Alice Geer. *Once the Hodja.* McKay, 1943.

Kendall, Carol. *Sweet and Sour: Tales from China.* 2nd ed. Retold by Carol Kendall and Yao-wen Li. Clarion, 1980.

Kennedy, Richard. *Richard Kennedy: Collected Stories.* Harper & Row, 1987.

Kipling, Rudyard. *Just So Stories.* Outlet, 1912.

Krull, Kathleen. *A Pot o' Gold: A Treasury of Irish Stories, Poetry, Folklore, and (of course) Blarney.* Hyperion, 2004.

La Fontaine, Jean de. *The Complete Fables of Jean del la Fontaine.* Translated by Norman R. Shapiro. University of Illinois Press, 2007.

——. *Fables.* Translated by Sir Edward Marsh. Everyman's Library, 2001.

——. www.fullbooks.com/The-fables-of-La-Fontaine1.html (accessed June 15, 2010).

Lang, Andrew. *Blue Fairy Book.* Edited by Brian Alderson. Puffin, 1975.

——. *Red Fairy Book.* Edited by Brian Alderson. Viking, 1978.

——. *Violet Fairy Book.* Dover, 1966.

Leach, Maria. *The Thing at the Foot of the Bed and Other Scary Tales.* Philomel, 1987.

——. *Whistle in the Graveyard: Folktales to Chill Your Bones.* Puffin, 1982.

Leodhas, Sorche Nic. *Heather and Broom: Tales of the Scottish Highlands.* Holt, Rinehart & Winston, 1960.

——. *Thistle and Thyme.* Holt, Rinehart & Winston, 1962.

——. *Twelve Great Black Cats and Other Eerie Scottish Tales.* Dutton, 1971.

Lester, Julius. *Black Folk Tales.* Baron, 1969.

——. *How Many Spots Does a Leopard Have? And Other Tales.* Scholastic, 1989.

——. *The Knee-high Man and Other Tales.* Dial, 1972.

——. *The Tales of Uncle Remus: The Adventures of Brer Rabbit.* Dial, 1987.

Lin, Adet. *The Milky Way and Other Chinese Folk Tales.* Harcourt, Brace & World, 1961.

Littledale, Freya. *Ghosts and Spirits of Many Lands.* Doubleday, 1970.

Lurie, Alison. *Clever Gretchen and Other Forgotten Folktales.* Crowell, 1980.

MacDonald, Margaret. *Five Minute Tales: More Stories to Read and Tell When Time Is Short*. August House, 2007.

———. *Peace Tales: World Folktales to Talk About*. August House, 1992.

———. *The Storyteller's Start-up Book: Finding, Learning, Performing, and Using Folktales: Including Twelve Tellable Tales*. August House, 1993.

———. *Three Minute Tales*. August House, 2004.

MacDonald, Margaret Read. *Twenty Tellable Tales: Audience Participation Folktales for the Beginning Storyteller*. Wilson, 1986.

———. *When the Lights Go Out: Twenty Scary Tales to Tell*. Wilson, 1988.

MacManus, Seumas. *Hibernian Nights*. Macmillan, 1963.

Manheim, Ralph, trans. *Grimms' Tales for Young and Old: The Complete Stories*. Doubleday, 1977.

———. *Rare Treasures from Grimm*. Doubleday, 1981.

Manning-Sanders, Ruth. *A Book of Ghosts & Goblins*. Dutton, 1969.

———. *Gianni and the Ogre*. Dutton, 1970.

Martinez, Rueben. *Once Upon a Time: Traditional Latin American Tales: Habia un Vez: Cuentos Traditionales Latinoamericanos*. Translated by David Unger. Rayo/HarperCollins, 2010.

Mayo, Margaret. *Magical Tales from Many Lands*. Dutton, 1993.

———. *Mythical Birds and Beasts from Many Lands*. Dutton, 1997.

McCarty, Toni. *The Skull in the Snow*. Delacorte, 1981.

McCaughrean, Geraldine. *One Thousand and One Arabian Nights*. Illustrated by Rosamund Fowler. Oxford University Press, 1999.

McCormick, Dell. *Paul Bunyan Swings His Axe*. Caxton, 1936.

Mehdevi, Anne Sinclair. *Persian Folk and Fairy Tales*. Knopf, 1965.

Miller, Dorcas S. *Stars of the First People: Native American Star Myths and Constellations*. Pruett, 1997.

Miller, Teresa. *Joining In*. Yellow Moon Press, 1988.

Minard, Rosemary, ed. *Womenfolk and Fairy Tales*. Houghton Mifflin, 1975.

Mincieli, Rose Laura. *Tales Merry and Wise*. Holt, 1958.

Monroe, Jean Guard, and Ray A. Williamson. *They Dance in the Sky: Native American Star Myths*. Sandpiper, 2007.

Olcott, Frances Jenkins. *Bible Stories to Read and Tell: 150 Stories from the Old Testament, with references to the Old and New Testaments*. Houghton Mifflin, 1916.

Osborne, Mary Pope, and Natalie Pope Boyce. *The Random House Book of Bible Stories*. Random House, 2009.

Pellowski, Anne. *The Family Storytelling Handbook*. Macmillan, 1984.

———. *The Story Vine*. Macmillan, 1984.

Pilkington, F. M. *Shamrock and Spear: Tales and Legends from Ireland*. Holt, 1968.

Power, Effie. *Bag o' Tales: A Sourcebook for Storytellers*. Omnigraphics, 1990.

Pridham, Radost. *A Gift from the Heart: Folk Tales from Bulgaria*. World, 1966.

Pyle, Howard. *Pepper and Salt*. Dover, 1913.

———. *The Wonder Clock*. Dover, 1965.

Rackham, Arthur. *The Arthur Rackham Fairy Book*. Chancellor Press, 1986.

Ransome. Arthur. *Old Peter's Russian Tales*. Puffin, 1975.

Reeves, James. *English Fables and Fairy Stories*. Oxford University Press, 1989.

———. *Fables from Aesop*. Bedrick/Blackie, 1961.

———. *The Road to a Kingdom: Stories from the Old and New Testaments*. Heinemann, 1965.

Ritchie, Alice. *The Treasure of Li-Po*. Harcourt, Brace & World, 1949.

Roberts, Moss, and C. N. Tay. *Chinese Fairy Tales and Fantasies*. Pantheon, 1979.

Robinson, Gail. *Raven, the Trickster*. Atheneum, 1982.

Robinson, Gail, and Douglas Hill. *Coyote the Trickster*. Crane Russak, 1976.

Ross, Eulalie Steinmetz, ed. *The Lost Half Hour*. Harcourt Brace Jovanovich, 1963.

Sakade, Florence, ed. *Little One Inch and Other Japanese Children's Favorite Stories*. Tuttle, 1959.

San Souci, Robert D. *Sister Tricksters: Rollicking Tales of Clever Females*. LittleFolk, 2006.

Sandburg, Carl. *Rootabaga Stories*. Harcourt Brace Jovanovich, 1951.

Sawyer, Ruth. *The Long Christmas*. Viking, 1941.

Schimmel, Nancy. *Just Enough to Make a Story*. Sisters' Choice Press, 1987.

Schram, Peninnah. *Chosen Tales: Stories Told by Jewish Storytellers*. Jason Aronson, 1995.

———. *Jewish Stories One Generation Tells Another*. Jason Aronson, 1987.

Schwartz, Alvin. *More Scary Stories to Tell in the Dark*. Retold by Alvin Schwartz. Harper & Row, 1984.

———. *Scary Stories to Tell in the Dark*. Lippincott, 1981.

———. *Whoppers, Tall Tales and Other Lies Collected from American Folklore*. Trophy, 1975.

Schwartz, Howard. *Elijah's Violin and Other Jewish Fairy Tales*. Harper & Row, 1983.

Segal, Lore, and Maurice Sendak. *The Juniper Tree and Other Tales from Grimm*. Translated by Lore Segal. Farrar, Straus & Giroux, 1973.

Shah, Idries. *The Pleasantries of the Incredible Mulla Nasrudin*. Penguin, 1971.

———. *Tales of the Dervishes: Teaching Stories of the Sufi Masters over the Past Thousand Years*. Penguin Compass, 1967.

Shannon, George. *More Stories to Solve*. Greenwillow, 1991.

———. *Still More Stories to Solve*. Greenwillow, 1994.

———. *Stories to Solve*. Greenwillow, 1985.

Shedlock. Ruth. *Art of the Story-teller*. Dover, 1951.

Sherlock, Philip M. *Anansi, the Spider Man*. Oxford University Press, 1988.

———. *West Indian Folk-tales*. Oxford University Press, 1988.

Sherman, Josepha. *Told Tales: Nine Folktales from around the World*. Silver Moon Press, 1995.

Singer, Isaac Bashevis. *When Shlemiel Went to Warsaw and Other Stories*. Farrar, Straus & Giroux, 1968.

———. *Zlateh the Goat and Other Stories*. Harper & Row, 1966.

Sleigh, Barbara. *North of Nowhere*. Coward-McCann, 1966.

Smith, Jimmy Neil, ed. *Homespun: Tales from America's Favorite Storytellers*. Crown, 1988.

Spaulding, Amy. *The Wisdom of Storytelling in an Information Age*. Scarecrow, 2004.

Stoutenberg, Adrien. *American Tall Tales*. Puffin, 1976.

Sutherland, Zena, and Myra Cohn Livingston. *The Scott Foresman Anthology of Children's Literature*. Scott Foresman, 1984.

Tashjian, Virginia. *Juba This and Juba That: Story Hour Stretches for Large or Small Groups*. Little, Brown, 1995.

———. *Once There Was and Was Not,* Little, Brown, 1966.

———. *Three Apples Fell from Heaven: Armenian Tales Retold*. Little, Brown, 1971.

———. *With a Deep Sea Smile*. Little, Brown, 1974.

Taylor, Margaret, comp. *Did You Feed My Cow?* Crowell, 1956.

Tchana, Katrin. *Changing Woman and Her Sisters: Stories of Goddesses from around the World*. Holiday House, 2006.

Thompson, Stith. *One Hundred Favorite Folktales*. Indiana University Press, 1968.

Timpanelli, Gioia. *Tales from the Roof of the World*. Viking, 1984.

Tolstoy, Leo. *The Lion and the Puppy*. Seaver, 1988.

Tyler, Anna Cogswell. *Twenty-four Unusual Stories for Boys and Girls*. Harcourt, Brace, 1921.

Uchida, Yoshiko. *The Dancing Kettle, and Other Japanese Folk Tales.* Creative Arts, 1986.

———. *The Magic Listening Cap: More Folk Tales from Japan.* Creative Arts, 1987.

———. *Sea of Gold and Other Tales from Japan.* Scribner's, 1965.

Undset, Sigrid. *True and Untrue and Other Norse Tales.* Knopf, 1945.

Vaës, Alain. *Reynard the Fox.* Turner, 1994.

Von Franz, Marie-Louise. *Creation Myths.* Revised ed. Shambhala, 1995.

Vuong, Lynette Dyer. *The Brocaded Slipper and Other Vietnamese Tales.* Harper, 1992.

———. *The Golden Carp and other Vietnamese Tales.* Lothrop, 1993.

Walker, Barbara K. *Treasury of Turkish Folktales for Children.* Linnet, 1988.

Wilde, Oscar. *The Happy Prince and Other Stories.* Dent, 1977.

Williams-Ellis, Amabel. *Tales from the Enchanted World.* Little, Brown, 1988.

Williamson, Duncan. *The Broonie, Silkies and Fairies: Travellers' Tales of the Other World.* Harmony, 1987.

———. *Fireside Tales of the Traveller Children: Twelve Scottish Stories.* Harmony Books, 1985.

———. *Tales of the Seal People: Scottish Folk Tales.* Interlink, 1998.

Winn, Marie, ed. *The Fireside Book of Fun and Game Songs.* Simon & Schuster, 1974.

Wolkstein, Diane. *The Magic Orange Tree and Other Haitian Folktales.* Schocken, 1980.

Wyndham, Robert. *Tales the People Tell in China.* Messner, 1971.

Yeats, W. B. *Fairy Tales of Ireland.* Selected by Neil Philip. Delacorte, 1990.

Yellow Robe, Rosebud. *Tonweya and the Eagles and Other Lakota Tales.* Dial, 1992.

Yep, Laurence. *The Rainbow People.* Harper & Row, 1989.

———. *Tongues of Jade.* HarperCollins, 1991.

Yip, Mingmei. *Chinese Children's Favorite Stories.* Tuttle, 2004.

Yolen, Jane, ed. *Favorite Folktales from around the World.* Pantheon, 1986.

NOTE

1. Orson Scott Card, *The Folk of the Fringe* (New York: Tor, 1990).

Webliography—Web Sites Useful to Storytellers and Students

There have been societies that did not use the wheel, but there have been no societies that did not tell stories.

—Ursula Le Guin[1]

INTERNET RESOURCES

Organization Sites, Including Listservs

www.healingstory.org (formerly healingstory.org@maelstrom.stjohns
.edu)
   Provides material for individuals working with those who are healing. Used to be a listserv. Now a more formal site, it requires mem-
   bership (accessed May 15, 2010).
www.storynet.org/index.html
   National Storytelling Network's site; formerly the National Storytelling Association. Includes what was storytell@venus.twu.edu (accessed May 15, 2010).

Indices

www.ruthenia.ru/folklore/thompson/index.htm
   Stith Thompson Motif-index (accessed July 15, 2010).
www.ilhawaii.net/~stony/loreindx.html
   Native American lore index (accessed July 15, 2010).

Modern Issues

www.snopes2.com/
Urban legends (accessed July 15, 2010).
www.darwinawards.com/index.html
Darwin Awards (accessed July 15, 2010).

Concerns/Ethical Issues

www.msu.edu/user/singere/fakelore.html
Folklore or Fakelore? Issues regarding stories rewritten to meet modern tastes (and sales) (accessed June 20, 2010).
www.hanksville.org/sand/sand.html
Cultural Property of Indigenous Peoples explains the need to protect Native American materials (accessed July 15, 2010).
www.wipo.org
World Intellectual Property Organization considers the rights of indigenous people in terms of folklore and artworks with a view to rewriting some of their guidelines on intellectual property rights of such traditional materials (accessed July 15, 2010).

Tales from Various Faiths

Some for telling, others just for reference. See also "Tales and Related Topics."
www.indianmythology.com
India—Hindu. Jatakas, Panchatantras, and more (accessed July 15, 2010).
ww2.netnitco.net/users/legend01/beast.htm
Catholic bestiary of tales (accessed July 15, 2010).
www.sacred-texts.com/index.htm
Many traditions, including Native American (accessed July 15, 2010).
www.sacred-texts.com/afr/mlb/index.htm
African tales (accessed July 15, 2010).
www.rider.edu/users/suler/zenstory/zenstory.html
Good, tellable Zen Buddhist tales (accessed July 15, 2010).

www.rider.edu/users/suler/zenstory/whytell.html
   Why tell Zen parables? Same site as above (accessed July 15, 2010).

Tales and Related Topics

www.pitt.edu/~dash/folktexts.html
   A first choice. Ashliman's work, includes tales as well as reference
   material (accessed July 15, 2010).
www.crystalinks.com/mythology1.html
   Links to many traditions & legends, particularly ancient ones (accessed July 15, 2010).
www.artistwd.com/joyzine/australia/dreaming/index.php
   Dreamtime legends (accessed July 15, 2010).
http://etext.lib.virginia.edu/toc/modeng/public/ZitLege.html
   Sioux legends (accessed July 15, 2010).
http://etext.lib.virginia.edu/toc/modeng/public/MclMyth.html
   More Sioux legends (accessed July 15, 2010).
http://etext.lib.virginia.edu/toc/modeng/public/LinIndi.html
   Assorted pourquoi legends (accessed July 15, 2010).
http://eawc.evansville.edu
   Ancient culture site. Many good connections, not primarily story
   (accessed July 15, 2010).
www.windows.ucar.edu/cgi-bin/tour.cgi?link=/mythology/hangman.
html&frp=/windows3.html&fr=f&sw=false&edu=mid&art=ok&cdp=/
windows3.html&cd=false
   Complicated to begin, but with lots of useful myths (accessed July
   15, 2010).
www.hawastsoc.org/deepsky
   Hawaiian site, astronomy focus, with short introductions to myths
   from various cultures (accessed July 15, 2010).
www.pantheon.org/mythica/areas
   Introductions to many myths from various traditions (accessed July
   15, 2010).
www.cs.cmu.edu/~bnagy/sarahsite/myths2.html
   Good overview folklore site (accessed July 15, 2010).
www.thorshof.org/zindex.htm
   Reference site for Nordic lore (accessed July 15, 2010).

www.sacred-texts.com/neu/kveng/index.htm
   Complete Kalevala—Finland (accessed July 15, 2010).
www.cln.org/themes/fairytales.html
   Various backgrounds (accessed July 15, 2010).
www.ilhawaii.net/~stony/lore98.html
   Excellent Native American tales, not all provide source (accessed July 15, 2010).
www.motherlandnigeria.com/stories.html
   Tales told in Nigeria, including various tribes and some European (accessed July 15, 2010).
www.users.globalnet.co.uk/~loxias/search.htm
   Answers questions about mythology and other classical subjects, includes myths (accessed July 15, 2010).
http://dianewolkstein.com
   Recorded stories (accessed July 15, 2010).
www.rickwalton.com/navlib.htm
   Source with many classic tales (accessed July 15, 2010).
www.aaronshep.com
   Storyteller's Web site, includes notes on stories (accessed July 15, 2010).
www.eldrbarry.net/roos/art.htm (also www.eldrbarry.net/roos/eest.htm)
   Teller Barry McWilliams's site. Older site, less formal, but with lots of useful information (accessed July 15, 2010).
www.pbs.org/circleofstories
   Native American storytelling with a few recorded tellings (accessed July 15, 2010).
www.fairrosa.info
   Look in the Reading Room for folklore collections. Also a good list of dragon stories and discussion of "Tikki Tikki Tembo" (accessed July 15, 2010).
www.courses.unt.edu/efiga/STORYTELLING/StorytellingWebsites .htm
   Higher education site with many references (accessed July 15, 2010).
www.youthstorytelling.com
   Kevin Cordi's site supporting young tellers (accessed July 15, 2010).
www.web.net/~story/mbstory.htm
   Some parables and other stories (accessed July 15, 2010).

www.timsheppard.co.uk/story/tellinglinks.html
   Site of British teller, Tim Sheppard, some links out of date (accessed July 15, 2010).
www.surlalunefairytales.com
   Collection of mixed tales (accessed July 15, 2010).
www.ucalgary.ca/~dkbrown/rstory.html
   Includes tale sites (Grimm, etc.) and some old books on telling (see Sara Cone Bryant) (accessed July 15, 2010).
www.storyarts.org/library/index.html
   Teller Heather Forest's site includes short versions of tales (accessed July 15, 2010).
http://dmoz.org/Arts/Literature/Myths_and_Folktales
   Links to many tale sites (accessed July 15, 2010).

NOTE

1. Ursula Le Guin, *The Left Hand of Darkness* (New York: Ace, 1969), introduction.

Selected Bibliography

It's never all in the script. If it were, why make the movie?

—Nicholas Ray, film director

Note: Most titles including stories are in the storiography or story collections lists.

Armstrong, David. *Managing by Storying Around: A New Method of Leadership*. New York: Currency/Doubleday, 1992.

Baker, Augusta, and Ellin Greene. *Storytelling: Art and Technique*. New York: Bowker, 1977.

Battles, Matthew. *Library: An Unquiet History*. New York: W. W. Norton, 2003.

Benjamin, Walter. *Illuminations*. Edited with an introduction by Hannah Arendt. Translated by Harry Zohn. New York: Harcourt, Brace & World, 1968.

Bettelheim, Bruno. *The Uses of Enchantment: The Meaning and Importance of Fairy Tales*. New York: Knopf, 1976.

Bettelheim, Bruno, and Karen Zelan. *On Learning to Read: The Child's Fascination with Meaning*. New York: Random House, 1981.

Birch, Carol. "A Storyteller's Lament: A Librarian Looks at the Rights and Wrongs of Sharing Literature Orally." *School Library Journal* (August 2007): 26–27.

Birch, Carol L., and Melissa A. Heckler. *Who Says? Essays on Pivotal Issues in Contemporary Storytelling*. Little Rock, AR: August House, 1996.

Blanton, John. "A Novel Medium: Hypertext Fiction Is Not a Great Art Yet, but It Is Creating a Whole New Way to Tell a Story." *Wall Street Journal*, March 28, 1996, R10.

Bly, Robert. *Iron John: A Book about Men*. New York: Vintage/Random House, 1992.

Bruner, Jerome S. "Myth and Identity." In *Myth and Mythmaking*, ed. Henry A. Murray. New York: George Braziller, 1960.

Bryant, Sara Cone. *How to Tell Stories to Children*. Boston: Houghton Mifflin, 1973[1915], http://etext.lib.virginia.edu/toc/modeng/public/BryTell.html (accessed May 15, 2010).

Campbell, Joseph. *The Flight of the Wild Gander: Explorations in the Mythological Dimensions of Fairy Tales, Legends and Symbols*. New York: Harper Perennial, 1990.

——. *The Hero with a Thousand Faces*. Princeton, NJ: Princeton University Press, 1968.

——. *Myths to Live By*. NewYork: Penguin/Arkana, 1993 (1972).

Campbell, Joseph, and Bill Moyers. *The Power of Myth*. PBS video series.

Carmody, Bruce. www.thestoryteller.ca/index.html (accessed November 15, 2009).

Checkhov, Michael. *To the Actor: On the Technique of Acting*. New York: Harper & Row, 1953.

Coles, Robert. *The Call of Stories: Teaching and the Moral Imagination*. Boston: Houghton Mifflin, 1989.

Collins, Rives, and Pamela J. Cooper. *The Power of Story: Teaching through Storytelling*. 2nd ed. Scottsdale, AZ: Gorsuch, 1997.

Colum, Padraic. "Storytelling, New and Old." In *The Fountain of Youth*. New York: Macmillan, 1940 [1927].

Dailey, Sheila. *Putting the World in a Nutshell: The Art of the Formula Tale*. New York: H. W. Wilson. 1994.

Danoff, Susan. *The Golden Thread: Storytelling in Teaching and Learning*. Kingston, NJ: Storytelling Arts Press, 2006.

Davis, Donald. *Telling Your Own Stories: For Family and Classroom Storytelling, Public Speaking, and Personal Journaling*. Little Rock, AR: August House, 1993.

Dayton, Tian. *Drama Games: Techniques for Self-Development*. Deerfield Beach, FL: Health Comm, 1990.

de las Casas, Dianne. *The StoryBiz Handbook: How to Manage Your Storytelling Career from the Desk to the Stage*. Westport, CT: Libraries Unlimited, 2008.

De Zengotita, Thomas. *Mediated: How the Media Shapes Your World and the Way You Live in It*. London: Bloomsbury, 2005.

deWit, Dorothy. *Children's Faces Looking Up: Program Building for the Storyteller*. Chicago: American Library Association, 1979.

Dundes, Alan, ed. *Cinderella: A Casebook*. Madison: University of Wisconsin Press, 1988.

——. *Interpreting Folklore*. Bloomington: Indiana University Press, 1980.

——. *The Meaning of Folklore: The Analytical Essays of Alan Dundes*. Edited and Introduced by Simon J. Bronner. Logan: Utah State University Press, 2007.

——. *Sacred Narrative, Readings in the Theory of Myth*. Berkeley: University of California Press, 1984.

Eastman, Mary. *Index to Fairy Tales, Myths and Legends*. Westwood, MA: Faxon, 2008.

Edwards, Carolyn McVickar. *The Storyteller's Goddess: Tales of the Goddess and her Wisdom from around the World*. San Francisco: Harper, 1991.

Egan, Kieran. *Teaching as Story Telling: An Alternative Approach to Teaching and Curriculum in the Elementary School*. Chicago: University of Chicago Press, 1988.

Eliade, Mircea. *Myth and Reality*. Translated by Willard R. Task. New York: Harper & Row, 1963.

Ellis, Elizabeth. *Mothers and Daughters, Daughters and Mothers*. Compact disc. Dallas, TX: New Moon Productions, 2001.

——. "Peddlar of Swaffham." American Storytelling Series. Vol. 2. New York: Wilson Video Resource Collection, 1986. Video.

Ellis, Rex. *Beneath the Blazing Sun: Stories from the African-American Journey*. Little Rock, AR: August House, 1997.

Estes, Clarissa Pinkola. *Women Who Run with the Wolves*. New York: Ballantine, 1979.

Evans, Ron. "Why the Leaves Change Color." American Storytelling Series. Vol. 7. New York: Wilson Video Resource Collection, 1986. Video.

The Fantasticks. A musical. Music by Harvey Schmidt. Lyrics by Tom Jones. 1960.

Forest, Heather, and Susan Gaber. *Stone Soup*. Little Rock, AR: August House, 1998.

Frazier, Sir James. *The Golden Bough*. 2nd ed. London: Macmillan, 1900. Available at www.gutenberg.org/dirs/etext03/bough11h.htm (accessed July 2, 2010).

Frey, James. *A Million Little Pieces*. New York: Doubleday, 2004.

Fulford, Robert. *The Triumph of Narrative: Storytelling in the Age of Mass Culture*. Canada: Anansi Press, 1999.

Geisel, Theodore Seuss. *Butter Battle Book*. New York: Random House, 1984.

Geisler, Harlynne. *The Storytelling Professional: The Nuts and Bolts of a Working Professional*. Westport, CT: Libraries Unlimited, 1997.

Gilbert, Elizabeth. *Eat, Pray, Love: One Woman's Search for Everything across Italy, India and Indonesia*. London: Viking Penguin, 2006.

Gillard, Marni. *Storyteller, Storyteacher*. York, Maine: Stenhouse, 1996.

Greene, Ellin, and George Shannon. *Storytelling: A Selected Annotated Bibliography*. New York: Garland, 1986.

Greene, Ellin, and Janice M. Del Negro. *Storytelling: Art and Technique*. 4th ed. Denver, CO: Libraries Unlimited, 2010.

Hale, Elizabeth. *The Peterkin Papers*. Boston: Houghton Mifflin, 1880.

Hamilton, Martha, and Mitch Weiss. *Children Tell Stories: A Teaching Guide*. Katonah, NY: Richard C. Owen, 1990.

Harrell, John. *Origins and Early Traditions of Storytelling*. Kensington, CA: York House, 1983.

Haven, Kendall. *Story Proof: The Science behind the Startling Power of Story*. Westport, CT: Libraries Unlimited, 2007.

Hearne, Betsy. "The Bones of Story." *Horn Book* (January–February 2005): 39–47.

———. "Cite the Source: Reducing Cultural Chaos in Picture Books." Part I. *School Library Journal* 39, no. 7 (1993): 81–83.

———. "Respect the Source: Reducing Cultural Chaos in Picture Books." Part II. *School Library Journal* 39, no. 8 (1993): 33–37.

———. "Swapping Tales and Stealing Stories: The Ethics and Aesthetics of Folklore in Children's Literature." *Library Trends* 47 (1999): 509–28.

Holt, David, and Bill Mooney. *The Storyteller's Guide*. Little Rock, AR: August House, 1996.

Hurston, Zora Neale. *Of Mules and Men*. New York: Harper Perennial, 1990.

Ireland, Norma Olin. *Index to Fairy Tales, 1949–1972*. 3rd supplement. Lanham, MD: Scarecrow Press, 1973.

———. *Index to Fairy Tales, 1973–1977*. 4th supplement. Lanham, MD: Scarecrow Press, 1989.

———. *Index to Fairy Tales, 1978–1986*. 5th supplement. Lanham, MD: Scarecrow Press, 1989.

Jackson, Michael. *The Politics of Storytelling: Violence, Transgression, and Intersubjectivity*. Copenhagen, Denmark: Museum Tusculanam Press, 2002.

Jung, Carl Gustav. *Modern Man in Search of a Soul*. Boston: Harvest/Houghton Mifflin, 1955.

———. *The Undiscovered Self*. Translated by R. F. C. Hull. Princeton, NJ: Princeton University Press, 1990.

Knuth, Rebecca. *Libricide: The Regime Sponsored Destruction of Books and Libraries in the Twentieth Century*. Westport, CT: Praeger, 2003.

Kroeber, Karl. *Retelling/Rereading: The Fate of Storytelling in Modern Times*. New Brunswick, NJ: Rutgers University Press, 1992.

Lambert, Joe. "What the Heck Is Digital Storytelling?" www.digiclub.org .stories.html (accessed June 24, 1997).

Larsen, Stephen. *The Mythic Imagination: The Quest for Meaning through Personal Mythology*. Rochester, VT: Inner Traditions, 1996.

Le Guin, Ursula. *The Language of the Night*. New York: Berkeley, 1985.

———. *The Left Hand of Darkness*. New York: Ace, 1969.

Leach, Maria, ed. *Funk and Wagnalls Standard Dictionary of Folklore, Mythology, and Legend*. New York: Funk & Wagnalls, 1972.

Lipman, Doug. *The Storytelling Coach: How to Listen, Praise and Bring Out People's Best*. Little Rock, AR: August House, 1995.

Livo, Norma. *Storytelling: Process and Practice*. Westport, CT: Libraries Unlimited, 1985.

Luthi, Max. *The Fairy Tale as Art Form and Portrait of Man*. Bloomington: Indiana University Press, 1987.

———. *Once Upon a Time: On the Nature of Fairy Tales*. Bloomington: Indiana University Press, 1976.

MacDonald, George. "The Fantastic Imagination," from *A Dish of Orts*. Whitethorn, CA: Johannesen, 1996. Available at www.gmsociety.org.uk (accessed September 28, 2002).

MacDonald, Margaret Read. *The Storyteller's Sourcebook: A Subject, Title, and Motif-index to Children's Folklore Collections*. Farmington Mills, MI: Gale, 1982.

———. *The Storyteller's Start-up Book: Finding, Learning, Performing, and Using Folktales: Including Twelve Tellable Tales*. Little Rock, AR: August House, 1993.

———. *Traditional Storytelling Today: An International Sourcebook*. London: Fitzroy Dearborn, 1999.

———. *Twenty Tellable Tales: Audience Participation Folktales for the Beginning Storyteller*. New York: H. W. Wilson, 1986.

MacDonald, Margaret Read, and Brian Sturm. *The Storyteller's Sourcebook: A Subject, Title, and Motif-index to Children's Folklore Collections, 1983–1999*. Farmington Mills, MI: Gale, 2002.

Maddern, Eric. *Nail Soup*. Illustrated by Paul Hess. London: Frances Lincoln, 2009.

Maguire, Jack. *Creative Storytelling*. Somerville, MA: Yellow Moon, 1992.

———. *The Power of Personal Storytelling: Spinning Tales to Connect with Others*. New York: Tarcher, 1998.

Marsh, Valerie. *Beyond Words: Great Stories for Hand and Voice*. Fort Atkinson, WI: Alleyside Press, 1995.

May, Rollo. *The Cry for Myth*. New York: Delta, 1992.

McLuhan, Marshall, and Quentin Fiore. *The Medium Is the Massage: An Inventory of Effects.* Produced by Jerome Agel. San Francisco: Hardwired, 1996.

Mellon, Nancy. *Storytelling and the Art of the Imagination.* Rockport, MA: Element, 1992.

Metcalf, C. W., and Roma Felible. *Lighten Up: Survival Skills for People under Pressure.* New York: Addison-Wesley, 1992.

Michener, James. *Tales of the South Pacific.* New York: Macmillan, 1947.

Mooney, David, and Bill Holt. *The Storyteller's Guide.* Little Rock, AR: August House, 1996.

Muth, Jon J. *Stone Soup.* New York: Scholastic, 2003.

NCTE. *A Position Statement from the Committee on Storytelling National Council of Teachers of English.* Available at www.ncte.org/positions/teaching_storytelling.html (accessed May 1, 2010).

Neuhauser, Peg. *Corporate Legends and Lore: The Power of Storytelling as a Management Tool.* New York: McGraw-Hill, 1993.

The New York Public Library. *A List of Stories to Tell and Read Aloud.* New York: New York Public Library: 1927–1990.

Niemi, Loren, and Elizabeth Ellis. *Inviting the Wolf In: Thinking about Difficult Stories.* Little Rock, AR: August House, 2001.

Noyes, Alfred. *The Highwayman.* Illustrated by Charles Keeping. Oxford: Oxford University Press, 1981.

———. *The Highwayman.* Illustrated by Charles Mikolaycak. New York: Lothrop, Lee & Shepard Books, 1983.

———. *The Highwayman.* Illustrated by Neil Waldman. San Diego, CA: Harcourt Brace Jovanovich, 1990.

O'Flaherty, Wendy Doniger. *Other Peoples' Myths: The Cave of Echoes.* New York: Macmillan, 1988.

Okri, Ben. "Aphorisms and Fragments from 'The Joys of Storytelling.'" In *Birds of Heaven.* London: Phoenix, 1996.

Orwell, George. *Animal Farm.* New York: Harcourt, Brace & World, 1946.

Pellowski, Anne. *The Family Storytelling Handbook: How to Use Stories, Anecdotes, Rhymes, Handkerchief, Paper and Other Objects to Enrich Your Family Traditions.* Illustrated by Lynn Sweat. New York: Macmillan, 1987.

Petress, Kenneth C. "Listening: A Vital Skill." *Journal of Instructional Psychology* 26, no. 14 (1999): 261–62.

Roberts, Judson. *The Road to Vengeance: Western Frankia Spring and Summer AD 845.* New York: HarperTeen, 2008.

Roney, R. Craig. *The Story Performance Handbook.* Mahwah, NJ: Lawrence Erlbaum, 2001.

Ross, Tony. *Stone Soup*. New York: Puffin, 1992.

Rovenger, Judith. "The Better to Hear You With: Making Sense of Folktales." *School Library Journal* 39, no. 3 (March 1993): 134–35.

Rumi. *The Essential Rumi*. Translated by Coleman Barks with John Moyne. San Francisco, CA: Castle Books, 1995.

Santillana, Giorgio de, and Hertha von Dechend. *Hamlet's Mill: An Essay Investigating the Origins of Human Knowledge and Its Transmission through Myth*. Boston, MA: Godine, 1977.

Sarnoff, Dorothy. *Never Be Nervous Again*. New York: Crown, 1987.

Sawyer, Ruth. *The Way of the Storyteller*. New York: Viking, 1942.

Schilbrack, Kevin, ed. *Thinking through Myths*. London: Routledge, 2002.

Schimmel, Nancy. *Just Enough to Make a Story*. Berkeley, CA: Sister's Choice, 1992.

Scieszka, Jon. *The True Story of the Three Little Pigs*. Illustrated by Lane Smith. New York: Viking, 1989.

Shah, Idries. *The Pleasantries of the Incredible Mulla Nasrudin*. New York: Penguin, 1971.

Shannon, George W. B., comp. *Folk Literature and Children: An Annotated Bibliography of Secondary Materials*. Santa Barbara, CA: Greenwood, 1981.

Sierra, Judy. *The Storyteller's Research Guide: Folktales, Myths and Legends*. Eugene, OR: Folkprint, 1996.

Simpkinson, Charles, and Anne Simpkinson. *Sacred Stories: A Celebration of the Power of Stories to Transform and Heal*. San Francisco: Harper San Francisco, 1993.

Sobol, Joseph Daniel. *The Storyteller's Journey: An American Revival*. Chicago: University of Illinois, 1999.

Spaulding, Amy. *The Wisdom of Storytelling in an Information Age*. Lanham, MD: Scarecrow Press, 2004.

Spolin, Viola. *Theater Games for the Classroom: A Teacher's Handbook*. Edited by Arthur Morey and Mary Ann Brandt. Evanston, IL: Northwestern University Press, 1986.

Sprug, Joseph. *Index to Fairy Tales, 1987–1992*. Lanham, MD: Scarecrow Press, 1994.

Stallings, Fran. "The Web of Silence: Storytelling's Power to Hypnotize." *The National Storytelling Journal* 5, no. 2 (spring/summer 1988): 6–19. Available at www.healingstory.org/articles/articles.html (accessed June 6, 2002).

Stone, Kay, and Donald Davis. "To Ease the Heart: Traditional Storytelling." *National Storytelling Journal* 1 (winter 1984): 3–6.

Stone, Richard. *The Healing Art of Storytelling: A Sacred Journey of Personal Discovery*. New York: Hyperion, 1996.

Sturm, Brian. "The Storylistening Trance Experience." *Journal of American Folklore* 113: 287–304.

Tan, Amy. *Saving Fish from Drowning*. New York: Putnam, 2005.

Thompson, Stith. *The Folktale*. Berkeley: University of California Press, 1977.

———. *Motif-index of Folk-literature: A Classification of Narrative Elements in Folktales, Ballads, Myths, Fables, Mediaeval Romances, Exempla, Fabliaux, Jest-books, and Local Legends*. Bloomington: Indiana University Press, 1955–1958. www.ruthenia.ru/folklore/thompson/g.html (accessed January 19, 2010).

Toelken, Barre. *The Dynamics of Folklore*. Boston: Houghton Mifflin, 1979.

Warner, Marina. *From the Beast to the Blonde: On Fairy Tales and their Tellers*. New York: Farrar, Straus & Giroux, 1994.

Willson, Meredith. *The Music Man*. Story by Meredith Willson and Franklin Lacey. First Broadway performance 1957.

Yashinsky, Dan. *Suddenly They Heard Footsteps: Storytelling for the Twenty-first Century*. Jackson: University Press of Mississippi, 2004.

Zane, John Maxcy. *The Story of Law*. 2nd ed. Indianapolis: Liberty Fund, 1998.

Zemach, Harve. *Nail Soup: A Swedish Tale*. Retold by Harve Zemach. Illustrated by Margot Zemach. Chicago: Follett, 1964.

Zipes, Jack. *Creative Storytelling: Building Community, Changing Lives*. New York: Routledge, 1995.

———. *Why Fairytales Stick: The Evolution and Relevance of a Genre*. New York: Routledge, 2006.

Index

accents, 44–45
accomplices in audience, 79
activities, 55–59
actors, 9–11
adrenaline, 72
adults as audience, 78, 103–4, 106, 134–35
advertisers, 124–25
Aesop's fables, 38
age-appropriate stories: for adults, 78, 103–4, 106, 134–35; for older children, 60–61; for teenagers, 78, 105–6; for young children, 55–56, 60–61
Anansi stories, 49–51
Angela's Ashes (McCourt), 19
anthropological versions of stories, 48–52
anxiety, 69–73
Arendt, Hannah, 139
Ariadne auf Naxos, 124
associations for storytellers, 84, 85
attention, need for, 76
audiences: connecting with, 13–18, 20, 25–26, 79–80, 94–95, 99; as listeners, 76–78; size of, 62; venues, 78–79, 82, 86;

willingness to pay, 83–85. *See also* age-appropriate stories
auditoriums, 82
authority, 79

Baker, Augusta, 57
ballads, 38, 65, 135
ballet, 118–19
Battles, Matthew, 127
Bauer, Caroline Feller, 57
bear tales, 101–2, 108n2
"Beth Gelert," 65, 135
Bettelheim, Bruno, 136–37
Biblical stories, 36
boa constrictor story, 39–40
books: displaying copies of, 66; e-books, 98–99; picture books, 56, 137
Broadway shows, 32–33
Brother Blue, 26, 83
Brown, Marcia, 65
Butter Battle Book (Seuss), 60–61

Campbell, Joseph, 103, 106
Camus, Albert, 101
candles, 57, 59
Card, Orson Scott, 179

Carlin, George, 86
categories of stories, 36–41
"Celestial Bear," 101–2, 108n2
Celtic tradition, 47
Cervantes, Miguel de, 93
characters, identifying with, 136–37
clarity of voice, 83
clowns, 15–16
collections of stories, 41–42, 53
Colum, Padraic, 47
connections with audience, 13–18, 20, 25–26, 79–80, 94–95, 99
consequences, unexpected, 136
cooking analogy, 110
copyright, 47, 97–99
costumes, 83
Coyote stories, 94
Creative Storytelling (Zipes), 92
cultures: learning from, 58–59; respect for, 41, 46–48, 53; versions based on, 48–49, 51, 64–65
cynicism, 104–5, 110, 121–22

Darwin, Charles, 91
Darwin Awards, 40, 123n7
Davis, Donald, 92
"dead voice," 28
de Beaumont, Mme., 41
de las Casas, Dianne, 86
Demi (Charlotte Demi Hunt Huang), 64
Dickens, Charles, 99
dog stories, 65
Don Quixote (Cervantes), 93
drama, 117
drolls, 39

ear and eye balance, 97
earth, connections to, 16

e-books, 98–99
Einstein, Albert, 135
electrician story, 120–21
electronic communication, 95
Ellis, Elizabeth, 27–28, 63, 86, 92
elocution, 72, 83
emergency back-up plans, 60, 66
emotions, 26, 117
empathy, 76–77
The Empty Pot (Demi), 64
Enclosures Act, 97–98
enunciation, 72
epics, 39
Erickson, Milton, 4–5
explanations during storytelling, 45
eye and ear balance, 97
eye contact with audience, 79

fables, 38
fairy tales, 36
familiarity of stories, 32–33
family stories, 92
fees, 83–85
Felible, Roma, 15–16
festivals, 28
films, 93–94, 135–37
folklore, 36
folk tales, 36–37, 40–41
freelancers union, 86
Frey, James, 18–19

games, 56–57
Geisel, Theodore Seuss, 60–61
Geisler, Harlynne, 86
Gerbner, George, 93, 95–96, 99
Greek myths, 102
Grimm brothers, 41, 48
group stories, 92

"Ha ha / Aha / Aaah" pattern, 63
hero tales, 38–39

The Highwayman (Noyes), 137
historical stories, 119
"The Hobyahs," 52
Holst, Spencer, 110–11, 119–20
Holt, Bill, 86
home venue, 86
honesty, 134
honor copyright, 47
hope, 4–5

imagination, value of, 107, 120,
    135–37
income tax issues, 85–86
indexes of stories, 41
individuality of style, 43–44
integrity in storytelling, 28–29,
    112–14
"interesting times," 67
Internet opinions, 96
Invictus, 104, 108n4
Inviting the Wolf In (Niemi and
    Ellis), 92

"Jack and the Beanstalk," 105–6
Jasser, Joseph, 3
Johnson, Jay, 69
jokes, 39
joy of storytelling, 14, 18–20
Juba This and Juba That, 56
Jung, Carl Gustav, 106

known stories, 32–33

language appropriateness, 45–46,
    61
Lansbury, Angela, 44
Larbi-Amoah, Stephen, 80n2
legends, 38
Le Guin, Ursula, 189
let down after performances, 72
libraries, 84

Lighten Up (Metcalf and Felible),
    15–16
listening, value of, 26, 56, 76–78
The Lord of the Rings, 39
loss, stories of, 125
lying within storytelling, 4

MacDonald, Margaret Read, 41
Mahler, Gustav, 35
Maier, Christopher, 18–19
"Man in the Moon," 65–66, 134
manipulation by storytelling, 104,
    124, 126–27, 135
mantra/prayer, 73
"The Master's Touch," 75–76
McCourt, Frank, 19
McGuffey readers, 93
McLuhan, Marshall, 97, 98
McWilliams, Barry (Eldrbarry), 43
media overload, 95–97
medieval tales, 39, 65, 135
memorization, 27–29, 52–53
Metcalf, C. W., 15–16
Micmac tradition, 101–2
microphones, 72, 79, 82–83
A Million Little Pieces (Frey), 18–19
modern fantasy, 39
Mooney, David, 86
Moore, Anne Carroll, 57–58
Motif-index of Folk Literature
    (Thompson), 41
"Mr. Fox," 135–36
mullah story, 116
music lessons, 25
myths, 16, 37–38, 102–3

Nail Soup (versions), 65
National Storytelling Network
    (NSN), 85
Native American stories, 37, 38,
    46–47

Nazi Germany, 127
Never Be Nervous Again (Sarnoff), 70–71
Niemi, Loren, 92
Nixon, Arne, 13
novel series, 94
Noyes, Alfred, 137
NSN (National Storytelling Network), 85
nursery rhymes, 61

obstacles and courage, 122
Okri, Ben, 18
online storytelling, 17, 93–94, 128
oral interpretation, 72
original stories, 52
outlines of stories, 31

Pacific Northwest culture, 37
pacing of stories, 63
parables, 38
participation stories, 56–57
Pausch, Randy, 81, 133–34
payment for storytelling, 83–85
perfection, 5
performance anxiety, 69–73
performance connections, 13–18, 20, 25–26, 79–80, 94–95, 99
Perrault, Charles, 41, 103
personal property, stories as, 37, 47
personal stories, 40, 92–93
Peterkin Papers (Hale), 29
Picasso, Pablo, 5
picture books, 56, 137
pornography, 128, 129n5
pourquoi tales, 37
prayer/mantra, 73
preaching, 9
printed words, 95, 98

programs: activities/props, 55–59; emergency back-up plans, 59–60; for larger venues, 62–63; themes, 63–66; time allotments, 62
property, stories as, 37, 47
props, 57, 59
Protestant reformation, 9
psychological aspects of storytelling, 106–7
puberty, stories of, 105–6
public speaking, 8, 70

The Queen, 6n3
questions, 77

raconteur tradition, 40
Ray, Nicholas, 195
reading as solitary, 93–95
recording stories, 31
religious stories, 47
repetition of stories, 31, 52–53
resources for professional storytelling, 86
respect for cultures, 41, 46–48, 53
responsibilities of storytellers, 11–12
room system for memorization, 30–31

Sarnoff, Dorothy, 70–71
Saving Fish from Drowning (Tan), 111
schools, 81, 84
Scieszka, Jon, 17–18
seanachie, 47
seasonal stories, 38, 46–47
Segaki, 91
self-stories, 17–18
sensationalism, 67
Seuss, Dr., 60–61

Singer, Eliot, 51
"Sleeping Beauty," 103, 105, 106, 134
sliding scale for fees, 85
smiles during storytelling, 79–80
songs, 38, 56
sound systems, 72, 79, 82–83
Sousa, John Philip, 25, 99
special circumstances, 81
spoken, compared to written, language, 46
stage fright, 73
standing-up stretch, 55
stealing from storytellers, 27–28
Stone Soup (versions), 64–65
stool for storytelling, 59
stories: known, 32–33; learning to tell, 26–31; selecting versions, 43–45, 48–52; types of, 36–41. *See also* age-appropriate stories
The StoryBiz Handbook (de las Casas), 86
storyboard notebook, 29–30
The Storyteller's Guide (Mooney and Holt), 86
storytelling: defined, 7–11; as gift, 8–9, 32; importance of tradition, 26, 91–94, 104–5, 119; responsibilities of, 11–12; stealing from, 27–28; styles of, 28–29, 43–44; teaching through, 107
The Storytelling Professional (Geisler), 86
Storytel listserv, 10
styles of storytelling, 28–29, 43–44
Sufi stories, 38, 116
Sunday schools, 83–84
suspense, 53

tai chi comparison, 109
tall tales, 39
Talmud, 109
Tan, Amy, 111
teapot song, 56
teenagers as audience, 78, 105–6
television watching, 93–94
Telling Your Own Stories (Davis), 92
themes, 63–66
Thompson, Stith, 41
"The Three Bears," 29–30
"Tikki Tikki Tembo," 51
time allotment for stories, 62
Toastmasters, 8, 70
"Touch of the Master," 75–76
traditions in programs, 59–60
Traveler (gypsy/Romani), 31–32
tribal stories, 98, 101–2
The True Story of the Three Little Pigs (Sciezka), 17–18, 46
truth, 4–5, 16–19, 112–14, 117
"Truth Found in a Peach Pit, 112–14
Twain, Mark, 55

urban legends, 39–40

values, 134
venues for storytelling, 78–79, 82, 86
versions of stories, 48–52, 64–65
violence, 52
visualizations, 29–30, 118–19. *See also* films
vocabulary, 77–78
voice projection, 71–72

Whitehead, Alfred North, 20
Who Says? (Birch and Heckler), 86
"Why Wisdom Is Everywhere," 50–51
Wilde, Oscar, 114

Williamson, Duncan, 31–32
Winfrey, Oprah, 18–19
winter-telling tales, 38
wisdom, 116–17, 122
wonder tales, 37
word-of-mouth advertising, 84
written, compared to spoken,
    language, 46

young children, 60–61

The Zebra Storyteller (Holst),
    110–11, 119–20
Zerbinetta, 124
Zipes, Jack, 92
zombie-like stories,
    27–28

About the Author

Amy E. Spaulding was born in San Francisco and raised in Vancouver. She began storytelling as a children's librarian for the New York Public Library and was the assistant storytelling and group work specialist for the system's eighty-plus branches. She went on to earn a doctorate from Columbia University. Currently, she is professor of library and information science at the Palmer School of Library and Information Science at Long Island University. She has served on many local, national, and international committees, advisory panels, and juries, including serving as a councilor for the American Library Association and chairing both the Caldecott and Notable Books for Children committees.

Spaulding has told for the New York Public Library in branch libraries, as well as at such locations as the Heckscher Oval of the Library and Museum for the Performing Arts at Lincoln Center, the New York Historical Society, and the Hans Christian Andersen statue in Central Park. More recently, she has lectured, served as advisor, and told stories for schools, churches, museums, and other organizations, such as NASA's Teacher Training Institute in Langley, Virginia, the Museum of American Folk Art in New York, the Rainbow Channel of Cablevision, and the Morrison Planetarium of the California Academy of Sciences in San Francisco.

She has published two other books with Scarecrow Press: *The Page as a Stageset: Storyboard Picture Books*, regarding the way picture books began incorporating elements of popular culture and can be viewed as a form of theater, and *The Wisdom of Storytelling in an Information Age: A Collection of Talks*, which won both an Anne Izard

Storyteller's Choice Award (2005) and a Storytelling World Award for special storytelling resources (2006).

Her storytelling classes are popular with students. In spring 2010, a student in her "Myth in the Information Age" class wrote:

> Dr. Spaulding, I really enjoyed your class. It made quite an impression on me. Out of all the college classes I have taken, graduate and undergraduate, this one was the most memorable and enjoyable. I shall never forget it. I hope you enjoy reading my paper, as much as I did researching and writing it. I must confess it is the only graduate paper I have written that I shared with my family to read because it was so interesting and not dull. . . . Have a wonderful Summer!!!!. Suzanne Kryger.